To Laurence,

Boldly go!

Happy birthday from Mike
and the rest of the crew

STAR TREK®

NEW WORLDS
NEW CIVILIZATIONS

STAR TREK®

NEW WORLDS
NEW CIVILIZATIONS

BY MICHAEL JAN FRIEDMAN

POCKET BOOKS

NEW YORK LONDON TORONTO SYDNEY SINGAPORE

POCKET BOOKS, a division of Simon & Schuster Inc.
1230 Avenue of the Americas, New York, NY 10020

ISBN: 0-671-88103-5

First Pocket Books hardcover printing November 1999

10 9 8 7 6 5 4 3 2 1

FOR DeFOREST KELLEY

FIRE

PART 2 :

WATER

69

AIR

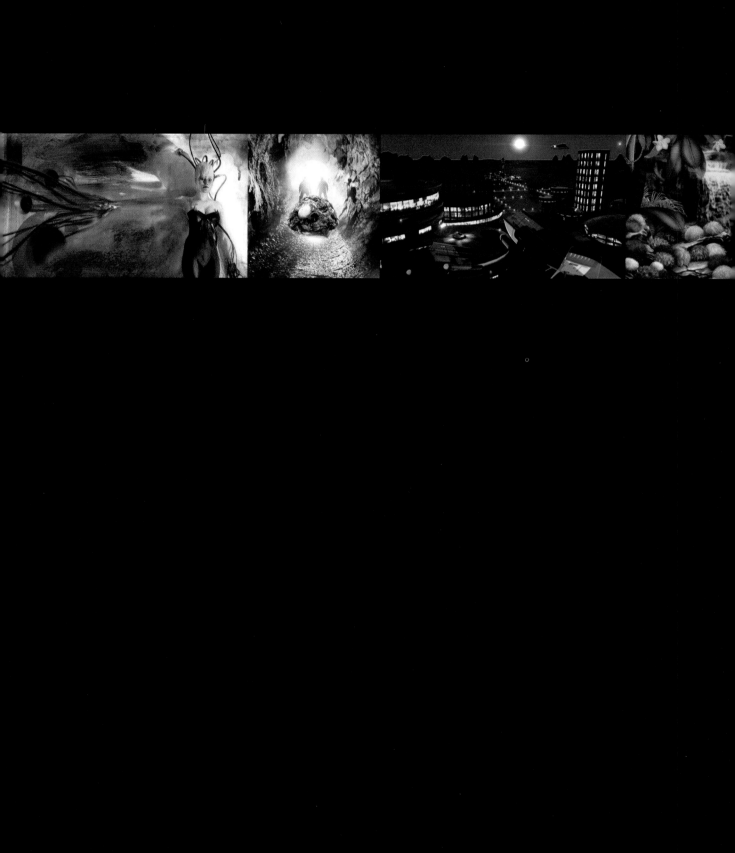

EARTH

A LETTER FROM THE EDITORS

For five long years we have felt the dogs of war tearing away at our way of life. We have sacrificed scores of our finest and too many of our innocents. Yet, we have held fast to one truth: We are citizens of a great community. We were not dominated from without. We chose, as sovereign worlds, as free people, to join the Federation. *We* have defined the ideals that have shaped our Federation.

What better way, then, to celebrate the end of the war with the Dominion than to look at these worlds, these civilizations, that make up the United Federation of Planets, both to reflect and to look beyond.

Realizing that we could not hope to cover all of them, the task laid before the editors of this work was to choose. But *how* could we choose? There are so many life-forms, places, and things, and they are all, each in their own way, important. Then, we were reminded of an archaic Earth belief. Fire, water, air, and earth were once considered to be the essential elements of the universe. Balance among them was "deemed" or "thought" to be essential. Once that balance was achieved, harmony would flow throughout the universe. So, in the spirit of that belief, we set out to choose our "elements." We sent out correspondents. Material was culled from both the Federation

News and the Starfleet News Division. We even delved into the logs of Captain Kathryn Janeway of the *U.S.S. Voyager*, transmitted from the distant Delta Quadrant.

Our next challenge was to decide how to visually represent these "elements." We could have sent out scores of holographers and the results laid before you would have been as pretty as any travelogue. But we wanted to see past the surface, look beyond the empirical. We wanted to see what no holoimager could show us: the intangible insights that come from experiencing these worlds and knowing their life-forms. To do this, we felt you needed the mortal touch, you needed beings whose lives and works have been shaped by living in the Federation. Artists were chosen and given rein to present their interpretations of these life-forms and places as reflections of fire, water, air, and earth. If what you see here does not seem entirely realistic, know that it does represent the reality of our galaxy, at its most elemental archaic level.

It is easy to get caught up in any celebration. However, this is a good time to remind ourselves of what we have been trying to preserve. Not just the Federation, not just our lives, not just our freedom—it is the right to travel freely among the stars, to seek out new lives, to forge new alliances, to expand our federation of worlds. And we must remember that these seemingly intangible ideals are not just our birthright, but the inalienable right of the inhabitants of every world and every civilization we have encountered and have yet to encounter.

PART 1 : FIRE

VULCAN
TEMPERED BY THE FORGE

It's *hot...*

Hotter than any place that supports life has a right to be.

Standing at the cracked red foot of Mount Seleya, wrapped in the finest thermo-lytic garments the twenty-fourth century has to offer, I still sweat so profusely that the moisture clouds my vision. I'm barely able to discern the outline of the mountain through my stinging eyes. Intellectually, I know the suit is minimizing my body's need to perspire, keeping me from drying up like a pressed flower. Emotionally, it's of little comfort.

Fire and ice: Even those who come prepared to cope with the arid heat of Vulcan's day can forget how cold the Forge gets at night, when the sun dips below the Kurat Mountain Range. At such times, desert travelers without shelter must fend off the biting wind racing in from the T'Kala Sea.

Here I am on one of the least habitable M class planets in the Federation on one of the most fiery days of its year, a parched and hapless human raised in what I now realize is the relatively balmy comfort of Earth's southern Arizona desert. For the first time in my life I understand the casual, if overused, phrase, "Hot as Vulcan." My native guide, Tavis, a retired master an impressive 220 years old, regards my discomfort with what I now recognize as wry Vulcan humor, though I know he would certainly deny the characterization if I were rude enough to mention it. His sole protection from the blazing star overhead is a simple white robe made of nothing more sophisticated than native plant fibers.

Surak, revered as the father of modern Vulcan culture, worked out the basic tenets of his rigorously logical

The Forge map

- Ancient Trails - prior to Time of Awakening.
- Transit way.
- ○ Historic site. △ Trailhead.

0 ——— 25 km

Legend conforms to Cartographic Standards of 2236

Great T'Kala Sea

THE FORGE

KURAT MOUNTAINS

T'Kurat Highlands

Mt. Seleya & ShariKahr

Tavis' Home

Temple

Statues

ShariKahr

Map conforms To Cartographic Standards Act Of 2237, UFP Regs. 3201.09 (Part 23)

Visitors to the Forge are frequently surprised that a region with so little surface water can support humanoid life (inset). But its proximity to the Great T'Kala Sea, where the planet's native life-forms are believed to have originated, may be the key reason that Vulcans hold the Forge in such reverence. It is a desert wilderness with links to a past that extends beyond living memory.

philosophy two thousand years ago as he trekked across the desert west of Seleya, a monotonously flat plane of sun-baked rock and sand that stretches for three hundred kilometers. Humans call it the Forge; even Vulcans will admit the logic of the metaphor. Maybe it's because so many of their children undergo a strenuous rite of passage on these sands, the desert tempering them, forging them into adulthood as their distant ancestors forged metal spears in the blazing heat.

When I first approached the Vulcan Consulate about crossing the Forge on foot they regarded me with skepticism. I insisted that my Arizona childhood had prepared me for the climate, but they "suggested" that I be accompanied by a Vulcan master of desert survival. I had casually assumed that with just a little technological boost, I could make a trek of the entire desert, end to end. Five days, tops. My hosts "proposed" that I start at the halfway point, the foothills of Mount Seleya.

As our hovercraft lifted off from the capital city, ShariKahr, I found myself captivated by the view. The complex, intertwining pattern of narrow streets at the center of the old city testifies to the Vulcans' longstanding preoccupation with mathematics and logic. As the city expanded, later architects, honoring the work of their predecessors, created intricate new designs in geometric harmony with those of the past. An ancient aqueduct system, one of the few relics predating the "Time of Awakening," draws precious water into the city from deep aquifers fed by desert hot springs some thirty kilometers to the south. Seeing it from this vantage, I was struck by the realization that ShariKahr is much more than home to eight million Vulcans—it's a continually evolving work of mathematical art.

As the city dwindled behind us, I was drawn to the unnerving image of T'Khut, Vulcan's airless sister world, dominating half my field of vision. Most humans never entirely adjust to the sight of its huge disk, ruddy and mottled by the planet's rich mineralogical diversity. T'Khut seems to watch over Vulcan like an ominous, omniscient eye, and it always seems so perilously, impossibly close. My mind flashed on the nightmarish thought that it could drop out of the sky at any moment and roll over Vulcan, flattening everything in its path. In reality, T'Khut's orbit is implacably stable. Mated by gravity, the two worlds are locked in a perpetual dance of tidal forces that stimulate the almost ceaseless volcanic activity common to both of them.

Only with effort did I force my eyes away to focus on the twin ochre cones of Mount Seleya that were slowly growing on the horizon. One of Vulcan's most striking and sacred geological formations, at first glance this barren outcroppings of sun-hardened sandstone gives no hint of the spiritual significance it holds for the people of this world. But as the lighting and the viewing angle became just right, I experienced a delightful epiphany: Mount Seleya's unusual outline mimics the customary split-fingered hand gesture used by Vulcans in greeting and parting.

Tradition holds that The Kurat Temple Complex at the base of the mountain was erected by Vulcan mystics over eight thousand years ago. The seemingly endless steps carved into the steep mountain slopes lead almost to the summit, where ancient ceremonies seldom witnessed by off-worlders are still performed.

To my disappointment, our hovercraft got no closer to the temple, silently vectoring off to an isolated bluff on a different slope of the Kurat mountain range. When I questioned our pilot about the course change, he responded simply, "Our presence would be disruptive." I took this as a diplomatic way of telling me, "*Your* presence would be disruptive."

We set down on a sunny rock terrace that is seemingly devoid of life, until the pungent, spicy fragrance of *favinit* invaded my nostrils. Its prolific, spiky petals extend from a slender yellow stalk that can rise as high as three meters. Most off-worlders find the fragrance produced in full bloom intense, to put it mildly. To my human senses, they reeked. But the pungent odor released by the billowing, translucent blossoms is typical of the flora found in the higher

Earth and sky seem
about to collide as
Vulcan's sister world,
T'Khut, rolls ominously
toward the zenith above
a terrain of astonishing
contrasts. Ancient foot-
paths and bridges carved
by volcanic forces and
pre-Reform Vulcans are
unique to this part of the
Forge. Priestesses from
a nearby temple see to
the ritual fires of the
ancient sites that dot
the landscape.

deserts, and a wide variety of popular spices are derived from the leaves of the *favinit* and other native plants. In the spring, fields of the fertile succulent cover tens of kilometers in the Surak province. *Favinit* roots sometimes burrow twenty meters below the desert caliche in their search for elusive water.

My pilot had already started walking toward a cave opening I hadn't noticed. Forgetting where I was, I ran to catch up, and immediately started to lose my breath in the hot, thin atmosphere. The pilot looked back, arching an inquiring eyebrow. I mustered as much dignity as possible as I forced my ragged breathing closer to normalcy. Before he could comment, I changed the subject. "Where are we going?" He resumed his climb. "To find your guide," he replied.

As we reached the cave entrance, I once again suspected the oft-denied Vulcan humor was at work. The interior of the cave was an ancient dwelling, so simple and primitive I found it hard to accept that anyone could still be living there. As my eyes adjusted to the dark, I began to make out the features of the oldest Vulcan I've ever seen sitting cross-legged on the red dirt floor.

A pair of surprisingly lively eyes looked up at me from a face lined and weathered by two centuries of desert sun. Tavis had spent all of his 220 years on Vulcan. He'd never once left his homeworld, not even for a brief visit to T'Khut or one of the orbital stations. "Vulcan is more than enough to occupy a single lifetime," he told me. I had trouble believing him. The

galaxy is rich with worlds whose diversity and stunning beauty boggle the imagination. How could anyone not want to leave his native planet and explore at least *part* of the galaxy? Tavis simply pointed to his head and responded, rather mysteriously, "All exploration begins and ends here."

The Vulcan Consulate had chosen Tavis to guide me across the Forge. He'd crossed it himself more than a dozen times, and in his orderly Vulcan mind he could visualize every meter of the terrain with photographic precision.

We struck out at dawn.

The Forge is a rocky, hardscrabble desert plain, with a scattering of sand dunes and a few spiny succulents sprouting here and there. Its southern edge is bordered by a sprawling system of mazelike slot canyons. Their exposed rock strata display an enchanting array of muted pastel colors, from rich, golden brown to sulfurous yellow. We head north, away from the canyons, toward the Great T'Kala Sea, which marks the Forge's northern border.

By mid-morning the intense sunlight feels as hard as the stony ground. Crossing over a small dune, we discover a jumbled pile of chalky white sticks. I come to the realization they aren't sticks, but bones. Tavis identifies them as the skeletal remains of a *sehlat*. Remarkably agile for such massive beasts, *sehlats*—two and a half meters tall with thick dark fur and massive limbs—are mostly found in the mountains, although they have been known to descend to the deserts at night in search of food. Presumably that's

Death comes easily on the Forge, especially when water is scarce. Skeletal remains found in the sand are not uncommon, particularly those of large carnivores unable to find prey. Here, the sun-bleached bones of an unfortunate *sehlat* testify to the constant struggle for survival.

Almost invisible against the sand, whirling "dust devils" move across the desert, the fierce winds sculpting the hard stone at the feet of the Kurat Mountains. Colossal red-crystalline statues of ancient Vulcan Masters overlook the Forge, as if contemplating the elemental drama that eternally plays out before them.

what this poor creature was doing on the Forge. Adult *sehlats* superficially resemble the ancient child's doll known as a "teddy bear," with the notable exception that *sehlats* possess six-inch fangs.

A handful of reptilian, avian, and mammalian species inhabit the Vulcan deserts and hill country. Sand vipers, common in the deserts, migrate south in the season that passes for Vulcan winter. We aren't likely to encounter one this time of year on the Forge, but Tavis tells me that migrating herds of the blue-green serpents can flow across the sand like a living river in search of a welcoming ocean.

We manage to cover twenty-five kilometers our first day. My exhaustion is mitigated by the exhilaration I feel at the amount of territory we've crossed. An impressive feat, I think, until Tavis informs me that on his last trek across the Forge he averaged sixty kilometers a day. Of course, he was a spry 114 back then. More Vulcan non-humor...

As we make our camp, I ask Tavis about the history of his proudly logical people. He tells me that the earliest Vulcan texts date back some 50,000 years. Prior to the "Time of Awakening," Vulcans were a highly emotional, violent species, almost constantly at war with one another. Some two thousand years ago, with their civilization on the verge of collapse, the revered philosopher and pacifist Surak convinced his people to reject their emotions and embrace a new form of mental discipline based on rationalism and pure logic (one of the contending factions at the Time of Awakening rejected Surak's philosophy and eventually left the planet to found the Romulan Star Empire).

Sunset on Vulcan is a blissful event. The temperature almost instantly drops twenty degrees. The harsh glare of the Vulcan sun is replaced by the cool glow of T'Khut. Here on the Forge, T'Khut hangs low on the horizon. Even though most of its disk is hidden from view, it still provides ten times as much light as a full moon on Earth. Tavis opens a packet of dried fruits and vegetables (the vast majority of Vulcans do not eat meat, even replicated meat). We eat silently, drink generous portions of water, then lay down on simple bed mats and prepare for sleep.

Halfway through our second day we enter the ruins of an ancient temple, a series of five-meter stone columns arranged in a wide circle. Tavis informs me that this place has been used for centuries to perform the *Koon-ut-kal-if-fee* ritual. Every seven years, Vulcans succumb to an irresistible drive to take a mate. During the time of the *Pon farr,* logic is cast aside and primitive, violent emotions once again take control. In ancient times, Vulcans fought for their mates in ritual combat, the grueling and bloody contest ending only when one of the combatants was dead. I've heard rumors that *Koon-ut-kal-if-fee* is practiced even today, although rarely and discreetly. For a moment, I think I see a wistful expression cross Tavis' face as he examines one of the stone columns. Did he himself once face a challenger in this sacred place?

On the fourth day of our journey, a line of swirling dust devils gathers below the approaching ridgeline, dancing across the sand like ghostly ballerinas. Situated on the ridge are the giant statues of the Vulcan Masters. At least twenty meters tall, carved from massive blocks of rubinitite crystals, they seem to glow from within, as if small pieces of the

Vulcan sun were trapped inside them.

It's easy to forget most Vulcans still possess emotions; it is not the existence of emotion, but its outward expression that is strictly forbidden. In each generation, however, a small number of Vulcans achieve the state of *Kolinahr*, complete freedom from all emotion. The Forge is where those who strive for this ultimate triumph of logic come to take their final test. Many are called, as the saying goes, but few are chosen. I'm concerned I may be violating basic Vulcan decorum, but I have to ask: "Have you achieved *Kolinahr*?" Tavis pauses before answering. "My path lies in a different direction."

The seventh day of our journey is the most excruciating. Just putting one foot in front of the other requires an extraordinary effort of will on my

As the afternoon sun begins its slow descent, Tavis points to a thin green line on the horizon: the Great T'Kala Sea, the northern border of the Forge. Another hour of walking and our journey is over. The highest frequency sonic shower cannot have been more rejuvenating than those green, brackish waves. My parched skin rejoices.

A hovercraft picks us up the next morning. Tavis and I exchange the Vulcan salute as he returns to his cavern home. "Live long and prosper," he wishes me, and I wish him the same, knowing full well he already has. As the hovercraft returns me to the shuttleport at ShariKahr, I begin to understand the degree to which the Vulcan landscape and climate shaped the Vulcan psyche.

"LIVE LONG AND PROSPER," HE WISHES ME, AND I WISH HIM THE SAME, KNOWING FULL WELL HE ALREADY HAS.

---

part. Tavis, however, looks like he's just out for a Sunday stroll. I remember the words of an ancient human writer, Samuel Beckett: "I can't go on; I must go on; I will go on." Every muscle in my body is on fire. But the ordeal of traversing this punishing landscape has had another, more significant effect on me. A distinctly Vulcan stoicism has begun to take hold of me. The pain becomes a separate entity, floating outside my body. I sense it, but I find I can also ignore it. Tavis seems to recognize this, perhaps through the limited telepathic ability common to all Vulcans. We press on.

On a gentler, less severe world, Vulcans would never have become so reckless or so bloody. But had they not been seized by violent passions, they would have never felt the need to master them.

The logic, it seems to me, is inescapable.

CAR

E verywhere I walk in the curved, low-ceilinged expanse of the ancient, stone burial vault, its contents illuminated by a series of humble tripod lamps, I'm dazzled by the kind of material splendor most sentient beings can only dream about.

On one hand, a four-legged predator with a narrow, scaled head stands over the carcass of a fat, horned herd animal—both beasts rendered in solid latinum. Elsewhere, a polished silver funerary mask, expressing a joyous serenity, lies face-up on a ceremonial table of dark *s'fajanah* wood inlaid with strips of bright red jevonite. In a third place, a vase carved from blue-veined volcanic rock imitates the generous blossom of the *kegopi* bush, which grows only on the highest peaks of the Opuuya Mountain Range.

A reliquary of this type was believed to have been buried with every monarch. This one is a magnificent example of the height of Hebitian engraving techniques. Standing over two meters tall, it is topped with a depiction of the ancient god of the underworld and a slumbering *toj'lath*. The fatted *toj'lath* symbolizes the monarch, and the god is seeking to wake the ruler for his journey to the next life.

DASSIA
THE GLORIES OF THE HEBITIANS

A shrine-chest made of intricately carved white *mastafh* bone overlaid with red gold is surmounted by a canopy of entwined ebony serpents. Jevonite statues of the four ancient death spirits surround the chest—each one an elegant female figure with outstretched arms, so fervent and devoted in their postures and their expressions that I almost feel the need to avert my eyes.

Oil-burning lamps made of gold are piled together, traces of oil still lingering in them. Silver belt buckles depict bountiful hunts and harvests that took place thousands of years ago. On an intricately carved chair, latinum-plated panels represent sleek, long-maned *zabos* drinking at a lake. A jevonite boat with a curved prow—the size of a child's toy—sails the waters of a bygone age.

And there's more. A good deal more.

Heaps of gem-encrusted armbands sprawl haphazardly, sparkling like dragon scales in the lamplight. Glittering necklaces and dramatic pectorals adorn almost every inch of the walls. Finely worked finger-rings that could each buy a year's supply of *regova* eggs are displayed in the rotting remains of round wooden boxes.

IT'S NO WONDER THAT CARDASSIANS LOOK BACK AT THEIR HEBITIAN FOREBEARS WITH A SENSE OF LONGING . . . . AND LOSS.

The chamber describes a continuous loop, beginning and ending at the same vestibular passageway. I'm told this is the first time this sort of layout has been discovered. I can't say from personal experience, however, because it's my first time in such a tomb.

As I admire these ancient treasures, I find it difficult to believe that I'm on Cardassia Prime. This trove of magnificent, jeweled artifacts seems out of place, not the handiwork of the austere Cardassians. Of course, they didn't call themselves Cardassians at the time of this chamber's construction.

In those days, they called themselves Hebitians.

The Hebitian Age, also known as the Age of the Five Kingdoms, was a golden one on Cardassia Prime. It was a time of peace and plenty that began some six thousand years ago and didn't break its stride for nearly four millennia.

But there's a good deal more than the passage of time separating modern Cardassians from their ancient antecedents. Where Cardassians are ascetic to the point of obsession, the Hebitians were in love with excess. Where Cardassian art is relentlessly didactic, Hebitian murals and sculptures were designed only to stimulate the senses. Where Cardassians pride themselves on precision and formality, the Hebitians were almost perversely spontaneous.

Though events have conspired to level the greater part of the Hebitians' once-proud cities, there's still enough of them left intact to give us an idea of what they looked like. The Hebitian capitals were undeniably glorious and exalted places, with bright, expansive plazas and graceful towers nearly thirty meters high, home to vibrant marketplaces and bustling seaports and one sprawling holiday revel after another.

It's no wonder that Cardassians look back at their Hebitian forebears with a sense of longing . . . and loss.

The air in the chamber is close and musty, with a faint metallic tang to it. But then, it was sealed until just a few weeks ago, when a Dominion energy blast uncovered its vestibule quite by accident.

The irony was instantly palpable to everyone who learned of the incident—that an act of aggression designed to crush the Cardassians should have revealed a prime relic of the Hebitian Age. The Federation suggested a joint effort to excavate the site.

So here I am, one of the first Terran archaeologists to set foot in a Hebitian tomb. However, it's not just the wealth of a bygone age I've come to examine. Of equal interest to me is the long, unadorned stone slab that serves as the focal point of the burial chamber.

I recognize it as the royal pallet. Unfortunately, all that's left of the Hebitian monarch who was laid to rest there is a scattering of bone fragments and a layer of dust. Foolishly, I place my hand over my mouth as I approach them, even though a forcefield now stabilizes the remains, determined not to stir anything.

Simple as it is, the pallet seems terribly out of place in the midst of so much glitter and extravagance. Of everything here, it seems more like the work of the spartan Cardassians than the prodigal Hebitians.

But then, from the Hebitian point of view, there was no more reason to adorn the burial slab than the body laid to rest on it.

The Hebitians didn't have much regard for a corpse once the life within it had expired. All they cared about was the soul of the deceased and how it would fare on the glorious landscape of the afterlife.

A great many other cultures have shared essentially the same view over the ages, the Klingons, the Anyorrites, and the Ebinda'sar of Xhonos Prime among them. However, it is difficult to imagine an afterlife as rich and bacchanalian as the one contemplated by the Hebitians.

All manner of earthly pleasures were thought to be available there in abundant supply, not to mention magnificent abodes and armies of tireless servants. There was only one catch—the spirit of the deceased had to pay for these perquisites, bribing the celestial spirits with cunningly wrought gifts of jewels and precious metals.

Hence, the prodigious quantities of wealth entombed with the king, so he could obtain whatever he craved in the life after death.

I have only one regret as I stand in the great stone chamber, surrounded by ancient riches—that I'm not likely to learn the name of the monarch who was buried here. Unlike the other Hebitian tombs that have been unearthed on Cardassia Prime, which seem to be substantially younger, this one doesn't bear any hieroglyphs to identify its occupant.

Suddenly, a second shadow joins my own, heralding the arrival of someone else in the stone vault. I turn and see that it's a Cardassian who has come in, but not one of the functionaries who brought me down here. For a moment, I'm at a bit of a loss.

Then I recognize the long-featured visage and the milky cataract over the Cardassian's left eye. This is my colleague, Chato Yuqar, with whom I've only corresponded by subspace until now.

OVERLEAF: Was this the true first face of the Galor warrior from which Cardassian society takes so many of its forms? Seen beside the dig-project supervisor, the mask evokes many of the distinctive details that are part of traditional Cardassian art.

"Glin Yuqar," I say, employing his title in the Cardassian militia, where he served as a young man.

Yuqar seems on the verge of smiling at my use of the honorific, which shows I've taken the trouble to learn about his accomplishments. But instead, he heaves a sigh.

"I'm glad you're here," he tells me, his voice taut with concern about something. Then he takes me by the arm as if we're old friends and guides me across the burial chamber.

There was no single event in Cardassian history to which one can point and say, "That's when the Hebitians fell." More accurately, the civilization of the five kingdoms faded over the course of long centuries.

Still, there were reasons for its decline. One was the depletion of the planet's resources, which had supported a growing population of aesthetes for thousands of years. Another was the rise of a worldwide ascetic movement.

This new variety of stoics called themselves Cardassians, which meant "people of discipline." Ignoring the ancient boundaries of the Hebitian kingdoms, their society came to revolve around extended families, where respect for one's elders superceded respect for one's monarch.

Cardassian historians have argued for some time over whether the ascetic movement came about independently or as a way of coping with their planet's worsening impoverishment. It doesn't seem that argument will be resolved definitively any time soon.

However, one point is indisputable: The Cardassians had a great many centuries of misery ahead of them.

"There is something here you must see," Yuqar tells me.

On the inner wall of the burial chamber, the Hebitians have stored a series of bejeweled shoulder ornaments, some bearing smooth, red chunks of jevonite and others faceted green gems that look a lot like emeralds. Slender links of chain dangle from each pale silver ornament, allowing them to be fastened to the wearer.

At first, I think Yuqar only wants to give me a closer look at the ancient epaulets. Then, glancing over his shoulder at the chamber entrance, he kneels at the base of the wall and uses his hands to apply pressure to one of the ponderous-looking stones there. To my surprise, it yields to my colleague's touch, sliding away over the smooth, flat stones of the floor until I can't see it any longer.

As my colleague turns to me, I try to understand what just happened. "There's an inner chamber?" I ask.

Yuqar nods grimly. "Come," he says, "I'll show you."

Then he snakes his way through the opening, moving with admirable agility for a fellow his age, and is lost to my sight just like the stone.

In 2167, a Cardassian farmer stumbled onto a Hebitian tomb in what was once the kingdom of Klu'haa. Before the discovery was a day old, the burial chamber had been looted by the farmer and his starving neighbors and its treasures exchanged for food on the black market.

Unfortunately, it didn't do them much good. They all died within weeks from a vicious strain of "viper's eye"—one of several deadly diseases that had ravaged their world off and on for several centuries.

The nearly bankrupt Cardassian world government began to excavate the surrounding countryside in the hope of finding additional tombs and artifacts. When a second burial chamber was uncovered, its riches wound up in the hands of the then-humble Cardassian Central Command, which used them to finance a foray against the people of a neighboring world.

The venture was a success. The defeated civilization's resources were seized and brought back to Cardassia Prime. More importantly, Central Command had captured the people's imagination, giving them something to take their minds off their troubles.

The excavations continued. And with each burial chamber that came to light, the military's power grew. In time, it had the wherewithal to pursue a course of aggression among the stars.

The stone, it turns out, is hollow. I can see that as I slither into the darkness of the chamber beyond.

Suddenly, a palmlight ignites in Yuqar's hand, illuminating the space around us. It's a smaller room than the one we've just left, its rounded walls bare of jeweled ornaments but remarkably full of the vignettes and hieroglyphs that have been discovered in other Hebitian tombs.

There isn't any treasure here. But there's another stone pallet, smaller than the first one, with bits of bone and dust on it. I wonder . . . is this the burial place of the king's wife? His child? Some favored servant?

My colleague beckons me and I follow him to the wall opposite our clandestine entrance. There are several scenes depicted there in the favorite Hebitian colors of blue and orange, their vibrance preserved by millennia of unrelieved darkness.

One vignette shows a trio of Hebitians throwing bits of paper into what looks like a ceremonial fire. Another shows a woman in childbirth, surrounded by midwives of both sexes.

"You see?" asks Yuqar.

Obviously, he's referring to something other than the pictures themselves, some significance I seem to be missing. "I don't think so," I reply.

Sighing audibly, my colleague points to one of the midwives. I look more closely . . . and I begin to understand.

For some time, the Cardassians had had their eyes on a world with a pronounced abundance of natural resources and a dearth of planetary defenses. In 2328, the Cardassian Union "annexed" this world—which was called Bajor—and began purposefully and methodically to ravage her.

Many of the planet's inhabitants were forced to flee. Those who resisted Cardassian occupation were killed or sent to labor camps.

Central Command remained a presence on Bajor

for several decades, lording it over the Bajorans. And as the supply of Hebitian wealth ran out, Cardassians came to rely more and more on Bajor for their daily bread.

But of course, Bajor's resources weren't unlimited either. And the Bajoran underground, with its relentless terrorist tactics, became a thorn in the Cardassians' side. Finally, after stripping Bajor of every benefit they could find there, the Cardassians withdrew from the planet in 2369.

Almost immediately, they found themselves with a homeworld rebellion on their hands. The evaporation of both Bajoran and Hebitian resources had thrown the Cardassian economy into disarray.

But as observers have been quick to point out, it wasn't just the Cardassian economy that suffered when the Cardassians left Bajor. It was the Cardassians' self-respect. After all, they had neither the Bajorans to look down on nor the Hebitians to look up to.

Without those familiar points of reference, it was easy for them to forget who and what they were.

S tanding in the small inner chamber and staring at the vignette that Yuqar has pointed out, I try to absorb the significance of it. It isn't easy.

"That figure is wearing an earring," I note. "The kind the *Bajorans* wear."

"Indeed," my companion says. He points to the picture again. "This is a birthing ceremony. Cardassians don't do such things. You see the instruments the midwives are playing? They look like Bajoran lyres."

I find that my mouth has gone dry. "So they do."

Yuqar moves to the next vignette—the one in which people are throwing papers into a fire. "This representation is very like the Bajoran Gratitude Festival. These papers could be renewal scrolls."

I take a breath, then let it out. It smells even mustier here than in the outer chamber. "If that's so," I say, "then the Hebitians . . ."

". . . could have been Bajorans. I know," Yuqar responds.

A few years ago, a Starfleet captain built a solar sailing vessel and took it from Bajor to Cardassia—whereupon the Cardassians admitted that they had discovered the wreck of a similar vessel.

Bajoran civilization is half a million years old. If the ancient Bajorans could have reached Cardassia, they could also have helped populate it. They could have made significant contributions to its most glorious era. Certainly, that's what these vignettes suggest.

"Who said this would be an 'easy peace'?" asks Yuqar. "My people are demoralized already. If this tomb indicates what it seems to . . ." His voice trails off miserably.

I nod. "It's a problem, all right."

The self-assurance of the Hebitian society is evident even in their wall decorations, as seen in this depiction of one of the many ministers who served this monarch. This was the agricultural minister; the chains to the worlds symbolize the close ties that the bounty of the earth had to his position.

Julianna Bass, the redheaded administrator of the Bersallis III research colony, glances at her wrist-chronometer and wonders where her son Anton is. "He was supposed to be back here nine minutes ago," she says, her freckled forehead creased with concern.

Twenty-year-old Anton Bass was dispatched to position a thermal deflector unit on a sandy ridge two kilometers north of the colony. Along with five other deflectors set up in a cross-connected, overlapping scheme, it's supposed to create a protective firewall against the grotesquely destructive firestorms headed this way.

ASHES, ASHES
BERSALLIS

We're in the outpost's gray-carpeted operations rotunda, which houses a series of curved, black control consoles: sensors, electromagnetic shields, life supports, communications. The overhead lights have been dimmed and the air is close and dense, small sacrifices that allow us to deploy more power to protective measures.

There's a hum of conversation permeating the place, though individual words are difficult to make out. However, I don't need to hear them to know what people are thinking about.

III

Gazing through a super-insulated, super-reinforced pane of transparent aluminum set above the control panels, I see a ruddy line developing between the sharp blue of the sky and the soft camel color of the mountains. The firestorm looks like it'll take forever to reach us, but at the speed it's traveling it'll arrive in less than half an hour.

If all the deflectors have been set up correctly, the colony will survive the storm intact. If not, our chances of survival drop substantially. But a human being left out on the open terrain of the perimeter, shielded only by the competing energy of the deflectors...

Along with Julianna Bass and everyone else in the rotunda, I hope that Anton and his team make it back before the storm hits.

Six years out of seven, Bersallis III is a reasonably generous host to the 640 or so Federation colonists who've made this world their home. Partway through the seventh year, it becomes a living hell.

That's when a buildup of particle emissions from the planet's sun creates a series of savage firestorms that rampage from one pole to the other. In the core of these extraordinary meteorological phenomena, temperatures routinely climb to 300 degrees Celsius and winds reach velocities in excess of 350 kilometers an hour.

For more than a century, these storms have followed a fairly predictable pattern. What's more, the colony was able to weather them without taking any unusual steps.

However, the last onslaught arrived eight months earlier than expected and exhibited twice the ferocity of anything that came before it—precipitating a call to a starship and the colony's first-ever evacuation. The storm we're facing now has materialized more than ten months ahead of time and its vital statistics are off the scale.

It's possible that this world is becoming too dangerous, that the Federation will have to abandon its installation here. If so, it would bring a remarkable research record to an end.

The Bersallis III colony was the first to measure the effects of high-atmosphere plasma on airborne flora, the first to synthesize diberylium from native ores, the first to identify seven different varieties of harmful bacteria. Year after year, its high-flying reputation has attracted the foremost scientists in the Federation.

But with the firestorms becoming more powerful, more unpredictable, that could all change.

"Some people think working at a research colony is romantic," says Niles Gutterman, a burly, gray-bearded exobiologist who's also one of the colonists in charge of the firestorm readiness program. "There's nothing romantic about it. You have to give up a lot for the sake of your work."

He looks out the window, hoping to see Anton Bass and his deflector team. There's no sign of them yet, though the firestorm is gradually eating its way into the sky. It's a pure, pale yellow at the horizon now, ascending frantically into shades of orange and red.

Gutterman glances at Administrator Bass, who's trying to distract herself by poring over a sensor panel, and scowls in his thick brush of a beard. "An awful lot," he mutters.

Like many of the colonists who've stayed here any serious length of time, Gutterman grew up at a Federation outpost. In his case, it was the research colony on Beta Canzandia, which was twice the target of Klingon raids before he turned ten.

"The people who do best here are practical and self-sufficient," Gutterman points out. "Those are qualities you develop when you've had experience with life at an outpost."

As I understand it, Julianna Bass grew up at an outpost as well—one that has since been turned over to the Cardassians. However, as I look at her face, I see there are some circumstances that no amount of experience can prepare you for.

Just three days before the storm began to gather, twin girls were born to Terran astrophysicists Lorraine and Marvin Laxer. They were the eighteenth and nineteenth "native" births on Bersallis III, a world without any multicellular animal life of its own.

As with all colony milestones, this one was celebrated with great intensity and in a variety of colorful

Seeing is believing: Safe within the observation post of the Bersallis III research colony, a scientist watches in awe as the fire wave races across the landscape, soon met by an array of instruments that will gather the most detailed data yet on this climactic anomaly. "Nothing prepared me for this. Nothing," she was heard to say afterward.

ways. The Laxers' Bolian colleagues showered them (literally) with gifts of precious metals—in this case gaudy red and silver flakes of tridianite and sorbomite mined from Bersallis III's vast mineral deposits. A group of Bajorans got together and sang birth hymns over the babies for twelve hours straight. And the only Klingon on the station, an award-winning meteorologist named Trohka, drank enough bloodwine to render herself unconscious.

another." On this day, all colonists are required to dress and behave as if they were someone from another species—preferably, one of the twenty eight represented at the outpost.

Another favorite is the Bersallin Music Extravaganza, during which everyone is invited to perform the most outrageous piece of music they can find on whatever instrument they care to come up with. Last year's Extravaganza Award went to a Gallamite who played

> ## "SOME PEOPLE THINK WORKING AT A RESEARCH COLONY IS ROMANTIC . . . THERE'S NOTHING ROMANTIC ABOUT IT. YOU HAVE TO GIVE UP A LOT FOR THE SAKE OF YOUR WORK."

But such occasions are few and far between, and they don't begin to break up the legendary monotony of life at a Federation outpost. Research in any venue can be a tedious enterprise; in a place without civilization or even a holodeck to mimic one, where living space is limited and supply ships only show up once every six months, the tedium can be downright painful.

To address the problem, the colonists hold a sporting event every evening before dinner—typically either Terran baseball or the Andorian game of *elan'tina*, which is similar to capture-the-flag. They've also made up some rather interesting holidays over the years.

One example is the venerable but completely fabricated festival of *Tuc'tu'tar*, which in the primary Tellarite tongue means "to wear the trappings of

a rousing series of Gorn victory chants on a set of Bajoran dinner chimes.

And so on.

Unfortunately, even a full slate of games and holidays isn't always enough to keep a sentient sane. That's why all prospective colonists must undergo a rigorous psychological screening—not only to join the outpost on Bersallis III, but to join any outpost in the Federation.

And even then, clinical depression isn't as uncommon as we would like it to be. Eight years ago, it led to the colony's first suicide—a case of unrequited love that claimed the life of a Pandrilite exobotanist. More commonly, it's led to carelessness on the job and a handful of potentially life-threatening accidents.

Ironically, the outpost has suffered more damage

from these accidents than from anything else—even the firestorms. Several outlying storage buildings still bear the black burn scars of a deuterium explosion that took place several months ago. The cause? Improper maintenance of a research vehicle by a depressed technician.

Clearly, morale is a major concern to everyone on Bersallis III. And it doesn't help that, in the back of your mind, you're always wondering when the weather's going to turn deadly.

Less than six minutes before the storms are expected to batter the deflector line, we catch sight of Anton Bass and his team.

They're running full-tilt for the shelter of the installation in their blue jumpsuits, a vicious, 500-meter-high wall of flame rising like a tidal wave just four or five kilometers behind them. Bass and another man are carrying shoulder bags full of equipment they were obviously reluctant to leave behind.

"Damn him," Julianna Bass mutters through clenched teeth. But her expression is unmistakably one of relief.

"Drop shields," says Gutterman, crowding the lavender-skinned Peljenite at the shield console. "Let them in."

The Peljenite complies and the colony's electromagnetic barriers are temporarily dropped. A moment later, Anton Bass and his colleagues sprint past the generator perimeter.

"Shields up," Gutterman barks.

Again, the Peljenite does as he's told. The shields are erected again, restoring the outpost's second line of defense. The rotunda hums like a beehive, as if everyone was holding his breath to that point—which may indeed have been the case.

Through the window, I can see the firestorm ravage what's left of the heavens, obliterating them with an all-consuming, red-orange fury. The technician at the sensor console tracks the storm's progress, announcing that it'll run straight into the thermal deflectors—a good thing.

"They're in!" a voice crackles over the comm system, partly broken up by the mounting proliferation of energy particles in the air.

But we all know what it means. Anton Bass and the others have entered the safety of the installation's main building. They're as well protected as any of us now.

"Two minutes," says the sensor technician.

I can feel my pulse race. The storm already looks like it's everywhere. How much closer can it possibly get?

The rotunda fills with the sour stench of sweat and fear. It's getting difficult to breathe. And still the firestorm approaches.

The turbolift opens and Anton Bass is there, along with a breath of cool air. He's tall and thin, with his mother's freckles. Wordlessly, he moves to her side and she puts her arm around him.

"We had trouble linking four and five," says the younger Bass. "Marz and I had to reset the wave emitters by hand."

His mother nods, but doesn't say anything in

response. She just pulls him closer to her.

"One minute," the sensor operator calls out.

We brace ourselves. I can hear the howl of demonic winds and see the fiery mouth of Hell open to engulf us. The temperature in the rotunda goes up another ten or twelve degrees.

The only question now is whether the thermal deflectors are going to be enough to keep the storm at bay. The life of every colonist on the planet depends on the answer.

"It's here!" the sensor technician announces, his knuckles turning white as he grips his console.

I glance at the sweaty faces of the colonists. They're solemn, drawn, as colorless as death. But not one of them makes a sound of dismay. They know they've done everything they can to safeguard their installation; the rest is in the hands of Providence.

A moment later, the storm buffets the deflector barrier with unimaginable fury, bringing wave after wave of superheated force. I can't believe anything made by man will be able to withstand such power. It seems certain that we'll be overwhelmed.

But we're not. Somehow, the deflector line holds its ground. The firestorm makes its way around us like a river of lava flowing around a rock, denied its quarry like every storm before it.

After a while, the intensity of the storm begins to decrease. The winds don't howl quite so loud. The red-orange flames start to falter, to yield to the blue of the sky.

"We made it," I think, then realize I've said the words out loud.

Julianna Bass looks at me, a grim smile on her face. "Did you have any doubt?" she asks ironically.

I smile back and shake my head. "None," I tell her.

In a matter of minutes, the storm is gone altogether. Of course, there could be others on the way, ready to spring on us without warning. But for now, the installation is safe.

As the temperature drops again in the rotunda,

we scan the terrain around the outpost. It's completely

black. Whatever grew there—a few varieties of scrub

plants and lichen—has been burned to cinders.

But it'll grow back. Life has a way of doing that.

Studying the firestorms as a potential energy source was but one of many objectives of Federation researchers. Alongside several observation stations, a line of thermal output sensors will measure variations in the storm's temperature and power over hundreds of kilometers.

KLINGON EMPIRE

A WARRIOR'S PATH

General Martok, the Chancellor of the Klingon Empire, submerges his goblet in a cauldron of bloodwine and raises it high so everyone in the smoky Hall of Warriors can see it.

Martok is surrounded by four mighty flames that leap from huge metal braziers. His one eye seems to dance in their ruddy light. As his lips pull back, they expose sharp, pointed teeth.

"To the Empire!" he growls.

"To the Empire!" a hundred throats rumble in response, making the stone walls around them shiver.

Then Martok drains his goblet and everyone present drinks with him, the rich, red bloodwine running down their chins into their beards. When they're done, they pound each other on their armored shoulders and butt each other with their bony foreheads.

The Hall of Warriors is a part of Ty'Gokor, the heavily armed orbital headquarters of the Klingon High Command. The occasion is Martok's confirmation as chancellor.

Normally, they don't allow off-worlders like me to witness such events. Fortunately, Martok feels a kinship with certain Starfleet officers with whom he fought side by side against the Dominion. When the Starfleet News

The chant of "Martok! Martok!" rings through the hall. It is a warm heartfelt welcome for this battle-scarred veteran of the Dominion conflict. Many of the warriors in the hall have served with the new chancellor, and there is talk of the glory that lies ahead for the Empire with Martok at its helm.

Service asked permission to give its audience a glimpse of the festivities, the general generously agreed.

I'm glad he did. This place is staggeringly barbaric—especially the four metal statues that tower over the warriors assembled here, vividly reflecting the firelight.

One is meant to resemble Kahless the Unforgettable, the warrior who united the Klingon Empire 1,500 years ago. A second is modeled after the Emperor Sompek, who leveled an entire city to save the Empire. A third reminds us of Ugilh, the hero of S'fajan Djag, and the fourth depicts Toldin, who held off the Federation forces at the Battle of Mordanus Prime.

However, none of these statues is as regal or imposing as the female who presides over the celebration, overseeing the distribution of *targ* haunches and the refilling of the bloodwine cauldron. Her name is Sirella, the daughter of Linkasa, and she is the wife of Martok.

Every now and then, she looks to the entrance and scowls. Having been briefed beforehand, I know she has good reason.

The province of Kentha is hot, humid, and full of big, black insects this time of year. Klingons who live here tend to remain indoors until the warm weather passes and winter comes, bringing some relief.

Nonetheless, there's a warrior walking the province's main road as if it were winter already, his long, brown hair falling proudly about his broad, white-robed shoulders. When he reaches a crossroads by a small,

marshy lake, he turns to his right and heads west.

Just a few kilometers from the crossroads, the warrior comes to a humble but sturdy-looking house made of large, dark stones. He's met at the front door by one of the house's retainers, who greets him with respect and invites him to come inside.

In the house's main chamber, the warrior meets the master of the place, an aged Klingon with white hair bound into a braid and two long wisps of a mustache. The warrior and his host embrace like old friends, though they've never met before face-to-face.

Then the master of the house shows his guest to a chair, takes another one for himself, and calls for bloodwine. It's brought by one of his daughters in a ceramic bottle bearing the ancient symbols for courage and honor. When the girl pours the wine, it flows thick and dark like the bodily fluid for which it's named.

The two men drink and wipe their mouths with the backs of their hands. Afterward, they put their metal goblets down and grin at each other for a while. Then the warrior asks his host a question.

The master of the house strokes his mustache and thinks about it for a moment. At last, he answers.

The cauldron of bloodwine has been refilled twice and still the celebration for Martok at Ty'Gokor shows no sign of diminishing. But then, an event of this magnitude can last for days.

Musicians arrive and take their places beneath the Klingon emblem on the wall. They beat their *krad'dak* drums and make shrill music on their long, slender *abin'do* pipes, stirring up the blood of the celebrants.

"His ribs cracked, his leg fractured, his heart true," the warriors chant. A song written about Chancellor Martok, who as a young man, **"single-handed slew the sabre bear. At the beast's death, this warrior cried out to warn the guardians of *Sto-Vo-Kor* that a worthy foe was at the gates."**

The warriors sing songs of valor and victory, moistening their throats with more bloodwine and stoking their fervor with handfuls of serpent worms. They engage in contests of strength and endurance, with the loser often ending up unconscious on the floor.

And still Sirella gazes expectantly at the entrance.

The wind blows fiercely on the uneven ground of Kang's Summit, bending the leaf-laden branches of the gray and yellow *micayah* trees. Overhead, great, gray piles of storm clouds slide across the sky.

A knot of hunters sits on a great, flat stone beneath the trees, fitting their dark, *tran'nuc*-wood bows with knotted strings made of *s'tarahk*-gut. As they work, they share a jest, but they're careful not to chuckle too loudly. After all, they don't want to scare away any sabre bears who might be lurking in the brush downslope.

In the distance, a twisted spear of white lightning stabs the horizon and thunder groans in response. But the hunters pay no attention. They've sniffed the air, so they know the storm will pass them to the east.

Suddenly, something moves upwind of them—and it's not just a *micayah* branch. Catching sight of it, they drop their bows and free the daggers at their sides. Their eyes narrow beneath their brow ridges, ready for anything, as a closer bolt of lightning illuminates the mountaintop.

Caught in the flash is a warrior with a white robe and long, brown locks. He glares defiantly at the hunters and their weapons as if daring them to come after him, though his hands are empty of weapons.

Recognizing him, the hunters snarl at each other with annoyance. One by one, they slip their daggers back into their sheaths.

As the ground shakes with the drone of thunder, they approach the white-robed figure with respect and even reverence—but he dismisses any difference between him and them with a gesture of disdain. Then the warrior poses a question to the hunters.

The hunters glance at each other, mulling it over. Finally, they tell the warrior what he wants to know.

The celebration at Ty'Gokor is going on its sixteenth hour. Warriors are howling with memories of glorious victories and even more glorious defeats. They regale their listeners with tales of the Romulans, the Cardassians, the Dominion, and the Breen.

Sirella, daughter of Linkasa, stands by the statue of Sompek and continues to glance at the entranceway. Finally, her vigilance seems to be rewarded. A powerful-looking figure strides into the midst of the revelers.

He looks around, his gaze stern, the corners of his mouth turned down in a scowl. Then, little by little, he begins to smile.

"Worf!" one of the warriors blares.

"Worf!" cries another.

"Worf!" roars Martok, loudest of all.

I know the name. Worf is the general's adopted kinsman. He's also the new Federation ambassador to the Klingon Empire.

Martok crosses the room and embraces Worf. Then, his arm wrapped around Worf's shoulders, the general leads him to the cauldron of bloodwine and fills a goblet for him.

Worf grins at Martok, then tosses back the bloodwine. A clamor of approval goes up from the assemblage.

The general's wife looks pleased at Worf's arrival as well. However, she doesn't move from her place by the statue of Sompek. And after a minute, she begins glancing at the entrance again.

The setting sun turns Lake Lursor into a pool of blood. Two figures walk alongside it, one a middle-aged warrior of proud bearing in a white robe, the other an older Klingon with plain garb and a thick, gray beard.

The volcano looms above them, an immense shadow against the twilight sky. Kri'stak has been quiet lately, not even bothering to rattle the cookware of the villagers in the vicinity, though it's been less than thirty-five years since an eruption made changes in the landscape.

Fiery red birds with hooked beaks glide across the lake, breaking its surface every so often to go after fish. When they get one, they fly it to shore and tear into it with undisguised zeal.

The wind is salty—not with the scent of Lursor, which contains fresh water, but with the briny flavor of the not-so-distant sea. The men breathe it in, their chins thrust out, their nostrils flaring.

Then they sing an old song—one that mentions the volcano and the lake and purports to explain the development of the *bat'leth*. But before long, the older man's singing turns into a coughing fit. His lungs are diseased, he explains, and he hasn't got long to live—a result of his exposure to plasma residue almost a decade earlier.

The graybeard has regrets, he says. He wishes he had become an officer. But then, he adds, that's the dream of every civilian laborer on every battle cruiser in the fleet.

The warrior asks him about a man with whom he served on General ShiVang's flagship many years ago. The older Klingon nods at the name. He remembers the man, he says.

Then he gives the warrior the information he came for.

In the city of Kling on Qo'noS, dawn is breaking with its customarily savage splendor. But here on Ty'Gokor, time's passage is measured only in the number of warriors who've passed out on the floor.

I've been smart enough not to sample the blood-wine, or I would certainly be among them. Instead, I've subsisted on the water and food rations I brought along with me.

Martok, whose eyes are hideously bloodshot, is leading a booming chorus of his favorite song. All those still standing are singing along as best they can, though it seems even to an alien ear that the lyrics are slurred.

Worf still looks as if he's got a handle on his senses, but it doesn't keep him from chanting as loudly as anyone else. And at the rate he's dipping into the cauldron, he'll soon be staggering as badly as the others.

Suddenly, I hear the sound of footsteps from the entryway. I turn and see a newcomer to the festivities—a burly warrior dressed in a white robe with long, brown hair falling about his shoulders.

Sirella eyes him like a hawk. Clearly, this is the individual for whom she's been waiting all this time.

Martok sees him too. As a hush falls over the Hall of Warriors, the general leaves his knot of friends and goes to meet the newcomer.

For a moment, the two of them stand chin to chin, appearing to size each other up. Martok is taller, but the Klingon in the white robe is broader. I get the feeling that they're about to fight.

But they don't. Instead, the newcomer speaks up in a deep voice. "I have traveled the length and breadth of Qo'noS," he says. "And I have spoken with those who knew you."

"Those who *knew* me?" Martok echoes, the slightest hint of suspicion in his otherwise amiable tone.

The newcomer nods. "I asked an old warrior named Sejokh what you were like as a boy, when you were growing up in the Kentha lowlands. I went to Kang's Summit to ask the brothers Abbakh and Kedjesa what kind of hunting companion you made. And I visited Mojjar of the House of Delagh to see how you comported yourself when you were a laborer on General ShiVang's flagship."

Martok's scowl deepens with each mention of his humble past, as if he's enduring a series of blows. However, he keeps his temper.

"And?" he snaps.

The warrior in the white robe eyes the general unflinchingly. "Sejokh said you weren't the brightest petal on the fireblossom, but you were always the most determined. Abbakh and Kedjesa told me you weren't very accurate with your bow, but you treat the sabre bears with the respect due a worthy foe. And as for Mojjar . . . he'll die singing of how you single-handedly turned back the Romulans."

Martok's mood lightens. His mouth twists into a grudging smile. "Have some bloodwine," he says, and he offers the newcomer his own cup.

Then the general grabs a new one off a table, dips it into the kettle and raises it in a toast. "To Kahless," he bellows, "who tore down the tyrant Molor, withstood the attack of the five hundred at Qam-Chee, and carried the day all by himself at Three Turn Bridge!"

"To Kahless!" the assemblage answers resoundingly.

Of course, it's not the Kahless of legend; I know that. It's just a clone of him created by the clerics of the planet Boreth. But to many of the Klingon people, this Kahless means almost as much as the original, so his word carries a great deal of weight with them.

"No!" the clone thunders in protest, his voice echoing wildly from one stone wall to another.

The warriors fall silent again, their goblets raised halfway to their lips. They look at each other, then at Kahless.

"Not to me," says the warrior in the white robe, "but to Chancellor Martok . . . scourge of the Dominion, slayer of Jem'Hadar!"

This time, the roar in the hall is twice as loud, eliciting a nod from the daughter of Linkasa. The Klingons empty their cups of bloodwine and shuffle over to the cauldron to refill them. And with that simple gesture, a new age begins.

Long live Kahless.

Long live Martok.

This hall is usually reserved for the presentation of the Order of the *Bat'leth*, and is dominated by massive statues that are rendered in the traditional Klingon style. In the hall's dim lighting it almost seems as if the chancellor is one of the ancient warriors come to life.

THE HUNTED
SAKARI &
HIROGEN

In my mind's eye, I can see the place as Captain Kathryn Janeway and Commander Chakotay of the *Starship Voyager* saw it. I'm in a lush forest of green fronds and orange blossoms, standing on a level stone surface that goes on for several meters until it disappears into undergrowth.

There are chunks of rock scattered about, some of them in piles as high as my waist, some only a little higher than my ankles. Once, they made up a building of some kind, a place where a sentient species lived in harmony with its environment. Now they're a monument to some historical disaster.

What happened here? Was there an earthquake? Or perhaps an accident involving the region's power source, the scars of which have long since been covered by nature?

Voyager's logs say it was neither of those things. In Janeway's judgment, this planet fell victim to an invader. And she has good reason to feel that way.

The elusive Sakari have adapted impressively to living beneath the surface of their world. Stealth, camouflage, and strict isolationism have come to define their culture.

Again, I use my mind's eye to picture a place. Janeway wasn't there, but some of her crewmen were. It's a subterranean cavern with a hole in its ceiling. A smoky yellow sunlight filters down, illuminating gray rock walls and snaking tree roots and a cascade of greenery where the light and an underground trickle conspired to nurture life.

I also see a pair of obelisks with alien characters inscribed into their tapering surfaces. And though they tend to blend into their underground environment, I see the denizens of this place who erected the obelisks.

They're humanoids with sharp-featured faces the color and texture of clay, though their black eyes are as hard and alive as river rocks gleaming in the sun. Their clothes and their headbands are gray and brown, the same as their stringy, uncombed hair.

They call themselves the Sakari.

Once, they lived on the surface, numbering in the hundreds of thousands. Then their civilization was attacked by a mysterious invader from space. The entire assault took less than an hour, but the Sakari were decimated. Those who survived did so only by abandoning their homes and escaping into the mines they had dug years earlier.

The Sakari never learned the identity of those who attacked them. They never figured out the motive for the attack either. However, Janeway and Chakotay uncovered a clue on the planet's surface.

It was the corpse of a Borg drone, its biological components deteriorated, reduced to its armor and its brittle, moss-covered bioimplants.

The Borg have made their impact on the Alpha Quadrant with tragic results. Anyone who lost a loved one at Wolf 359 can attest to that.

However, their impact on the Delta Quadrant, where they appear to have originated, has been many times greater. If the data we received from *Voyager* is at all accurate, the Borg collective has assimilated thousands of sentient species there.

But are their methods the same in the Delta Quadrant as they are here? Have they changed over the years? Have the Borg *themselves* changed?

These were some of the questions I wished to address when I petitioned the Federation Security Commission for academic research access to the *Voyager* logs. When permission was granted, I immediately set to work trying to identify the oldest incident of Borg invasion available.

The one I finally settled on took place no less than 110,000 years ago. In fact, it may have been one of the collective's earliest conquests, though that's just conjecture on my part.

Of course, the crew of *Voyager* encountered this species as well. However, they didn't seem to be aware that it had ever been victimized by the Borg. At least, that was the impression I got from their logs.

It's easy to see how they might have been misled at first. The species in question was powerful, numerous, remarkably aggressive in its own right. It seemed more likely to conquer than to be conquered.

Besides, Janeway's logs made it clear, she knew the Borg are nothing if not thorough. They don't often leave unassimilated survivors in their wake . . . which made the Sakari situation seem even more intriguing to me.

And yet, these particular conquerors *had* been conquered. This information was represented quite clearly in *Voyager*'s database. So why did it seem that Janeway and her officers were ignorant of the fact?

It took me a while, but I finally figured it out. The data on the conqueror-species wasn't originally part of the holographic datastream that Janeway sent to the Alpha Quadrant. It was inadvertently added to the stream by one of the alien relay stations involved in the process.

How is it that the relay station contained data on the conqueror-species? As it turns out, it was the conqueror-species who built the relay network more than a hundred millennia ago.

The species' name for itself was *Hirogen*.

I close my eyes, but not to see the planet of the Sakari again. This time, I see a fleet of ships knifing through the void—hundreds, perhaps thousands of iridescent blue vessels with elegant lines and graceful, sweeping warp nacelles. Their lizardlike occupants are running away from their homeworld, abandoning it in the interest of survival, because they know that a Borg cube is coming to assimilate anyone left.

And there *are* Hirogen who have remained—those who believe they can stave off the collective despite everything they've learned about it, those willing to defend their homes at any cost. There's no hope for these Hirogen, of course. They're completely and utterly doomed.

For those who've taken flight, however, there's a good deal of hope. There's an opportunity to preserve the virtues of their civilization, which have become considerable.

Unfortunately, even these Hirogen haven't escaped the Borg unscathed. They've become reluctant nomads, their souls scarred by the knowledge that there was a force in the universe powerful enough to destroy them—a force they may meet again some day. In each of their ships, they vow never again to play the role of the hunted. From that time on, they say with emotion in their voices, the Hirogen will become the hunters.

And they do.

They develop ultra-strong body armor and fearsome handheld particle weapons. They abandon the slender grace of their ancient ship designs, manufacturing massive, monotanium-plated vessels with dicyclic warp engines capable of traversing huge distances. They breed their young for height and muscle mass and endurance, with immune systems that can neutralize almost any kind of poison imaginable.

Everything the Hirogen do, every iota of energy they expend, is designed to enhance their people's efficiency as predators. All aspects of their culture come to revolve about the hunt . . . their arts, their sciences, even their religion. It pays off in one successful expedition after another.

But so dedicated are the Hirogen, so expert at their chosen activity, it becomes increasingly difficult for them to find a species who can pose a challenge

A Borg scout ship is caught in the final stages of the hunt. Prized above every trophy, a Hirogen hunter can become an Alpha Hirogen with one simple capture — the skeleton of a Borg. Destruction of this ship forced the hunter team to the planet surface and into the collective nightmares of the Sakari.

to them. So their armada begins to split up into smaller packs and ultimately into a far-flung array of lone vessels, each one competing with the others for the honor of the most impressive kill.

But they don't give up their ability to exchange information with each other, because that would weaken them as a species. In fact, they go to great lengths to create a network of powerful communications relay stations fueled by harnessed micro-singularities.

torture chamber. Metal blades and vicious-looking probes hang from hooks and chains anchored in the ceiling. Nets contain as-yet-unprocessed body parts, waiting to be denatured in transparent tanks full of green liquid. The bulkheads are decorated with skulls and spines and internal organs ripped from the living, thrashing bodies of the Hirogen's helpless victims.

It serves as graphic evidence of the Hirogen's prowess as hunters. But no matter how many trophies

THEY'VE BECOME RELUCTANT NOMADS, THEIR SOULS SCARRED BY THE KNOWLEDGE THAT THERE WAS A FORCE IN THE UNIVERSE POWERFUL ENOUGH TO DESTROY THEM...

Over the span of more than a hundred millennia, the Hirogen lose the details of their flight from their homeworld. They forget exactly who it was that they feared. And yet, the trauma of the event continues to drive their need for prey.

They adopt primitive rituals and practices. They start daubing their metallic headgear with hunt colors— white to signify dominance and leadership, red to signify loyalty and obedience. Their victims are daubed as well when possible, their alien faces marked with blue for imminent death.

Even more bizarre is the Hirogen's practice of stocking their cargo holds with grisly trophies of the quarry they've run to earth. If I try, I can picture the hold in which two of Janeway's crewmen were held.

To my human sensibilities, it seems like a medieval

they amass, no matter how many innocent aliens they eviscerate, it's never enough.

Because even if they've forgotten the minutiae of their flight from the Borg, they still know in the dark, dim depths of their blood that there's a force they've yet to overcome, an enemy that sent them running for their lives a long, long time ago . . .

And who may try to do it again someday.

The memories of the Hirogen might have dimmed over the years, but the relay stations remembered with uncanny precision. Powered by the energy of collapsed suns, they retained every scrap of information that had passed from one of them to another since the day they were built.

Quite clearly, they recalled the Borg.

But from what I've been able to gather, the Hirogen seemed disdainful of this resource. They used the

If the Hirogen only knew. Their societal ritual comes not from their ancient culture but is instead the by-product of the attempted assimilation by the Borg. The only clothing the Hirogen wear is armor, which resembles the stripped and fused bones of many hunts. Could this have been donned first as protection from the cutting tools of Borg drones?

relay stations only to transmit tactical messages, ignoring the network's greater potential.

That's why the hunters who captured two of *Voyager*'s people didn't identify one of them as a former Borg, a drone whom Janeway had rescued months earlier. Anyone at all familiar with the collective would have recognized the distinctive nature of the drone's implants.

But the Hirogen hunt-leader didn't see anything unusual about them. In fact, he perceived the drone and her Vulcan companion as two members of the same prey-species, indistinguishable from one another except for the difference in their sexes.

Nor did he realize that one of his brother hunters had already taken a Borg trophy decades earlier.

In my mind's eye, I see a Borg scout vessel—a dark cube one-hundredth the size of a regular Borg ship. The scout is sparking, venting clouds of white-hot plasma, enduring electromagnetic lightnings that race across the surface of its hull like parasites.

The scout is dying.

It was damaged initially in some incident of which the relay network is unaware. Even then, the cube might have limped across space to rejoin its mothership. However, it has the bad fortune to run across the sensor grid of a Hirogen hunt-leader.

I picture the hunter ship closing with the Borg vessel at the edge of a solar system and considering his short-range sensor data. The scout won't put up much of a fight in its present condition, it seems to

the hunt-leader. However, it contains beings of a sort he's never seen before. Eventually, the uniqueness of the relics he hopes to obtain outweighs his contempt for his prey's defensive abilities.

Bringing his particle weapons to bear, he disables the few systems that still function on the scout. Then he attempts to transport the crew of five onto his vessel.

Unfortunately for the hunter as well as his intended prey, there's too much energy running rampant on the Borg ship for the Hirogen to get a secure lock on them. What's more, the scout is headed for a collision with one of the system's outermost worlds, and the hunter is reluctant to deploy a tractor beam for fear his prey will explode in his face.

So he does what any experienced hunter would do—he takes a reasonable chance. He deploys additional power to his shields and remains close enough to try to obtain a transporter lock.

As the Borg vessel pierces the planet's outer atmosphere, the Hirogen finally succeeds in his efforts. However, his success is only momentary, because the scout chooses that moment to erupt in a paroxysm of antimatter fury. The Hirogen ship is unharmed, though the transport has been interrupted and the hunt along with it.

But according to the account the hunter will later send through the relay network, the five Borg were held in his pattern buffer long enough to protect them from the blast. That means they might still be alive somewhere on the planet's surface.

Arming himself and a handful of his subordinates,

Driven by their cultural mores, the Hirogen see first contact only as an opportunity for capturing unique prey and displaying horrific trophies. There is no attempt at communication, no room for negotiation, making them, in many ways, very similiar to the Borg.

the hunter daubs his headgear with white paint and beams down after his prey. When he arrives, he finds himself standing in the midst of fiery devastation—the result of the scout ship's rather impressive explosion.

Fortunately for the hunters, their body armor and rebreathing apparatuses protect them from the fires and the radioactive fallout, and their immune systems nullify what their armor can't keep out. At their leader's command, they fan out and search for the scout's occupants.

After several hours, they find two of the Borg. There's not much left of them besides charred bones and metal components, but it's enough for the hunt-leader to hang on his bulkhead.

What's more, he's discovered a bonus—a pack of the planet's native sentients, who were apparently driven from their homes by the blast. The hunt-leader picks out two to bring back to his vessel for evisceration. He orders the rest of them killed out of hand, an assignment that his subordinates are quick to carry out.

Then the Hirogen and their quarry beam back to their vessel, where the hunt-leader intends to gut his living prizes. But first, he asks them about their people and their culture. They say their civilization is a peaceful one, devoted to art and philosophy.

They call themselves *Sakari*.

It took me more than a year to uncover the truth . . . to see that, contrary to the evidence unearthed by Janeway and Chakotay, the Borg hadn't come to the Sakari's homeworld to assimilate them. A scout ship had crashed there because the Hirogen were, in effect, trying to assimilate the Borg.

In fact, if anyone could be blamed for the destruction of Sakari civilization, it was the Hirogen. And the only reason they hunted the Borg was because the Borg hunted them more than a hundred millennia earlier.

Ironies upon ironies.

And with the relay system no longer functioning for a reason I can't fathom, neither the Borg nor the Hirogen nor the Sakari are likely to learn how intertwined their destinies have been.

That knowledge has been the sole province of a single humble exosociologist in a research facility in Cleveland. But now I can share it with the rest of the Federation.

And maybe with a little luck, I'll be able to share it with the crew of *Voyager* someday as well. ◉

Left behind, this drone inspired terror in an entire society, something that the inhabitants of Earth and the survivors of Wolf 359 can well understand.

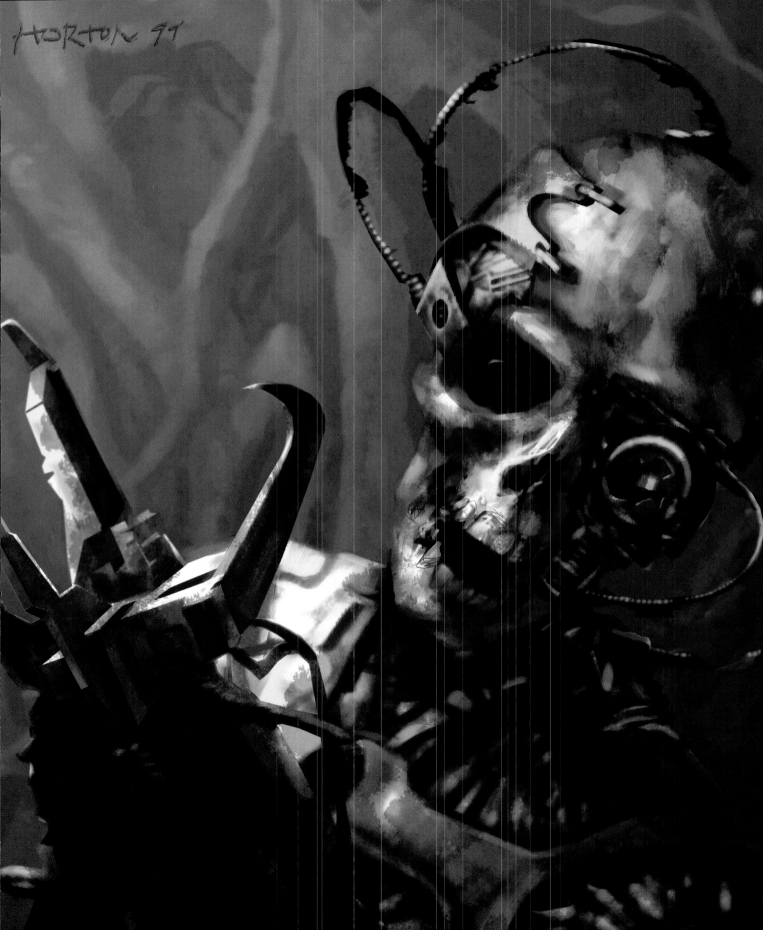

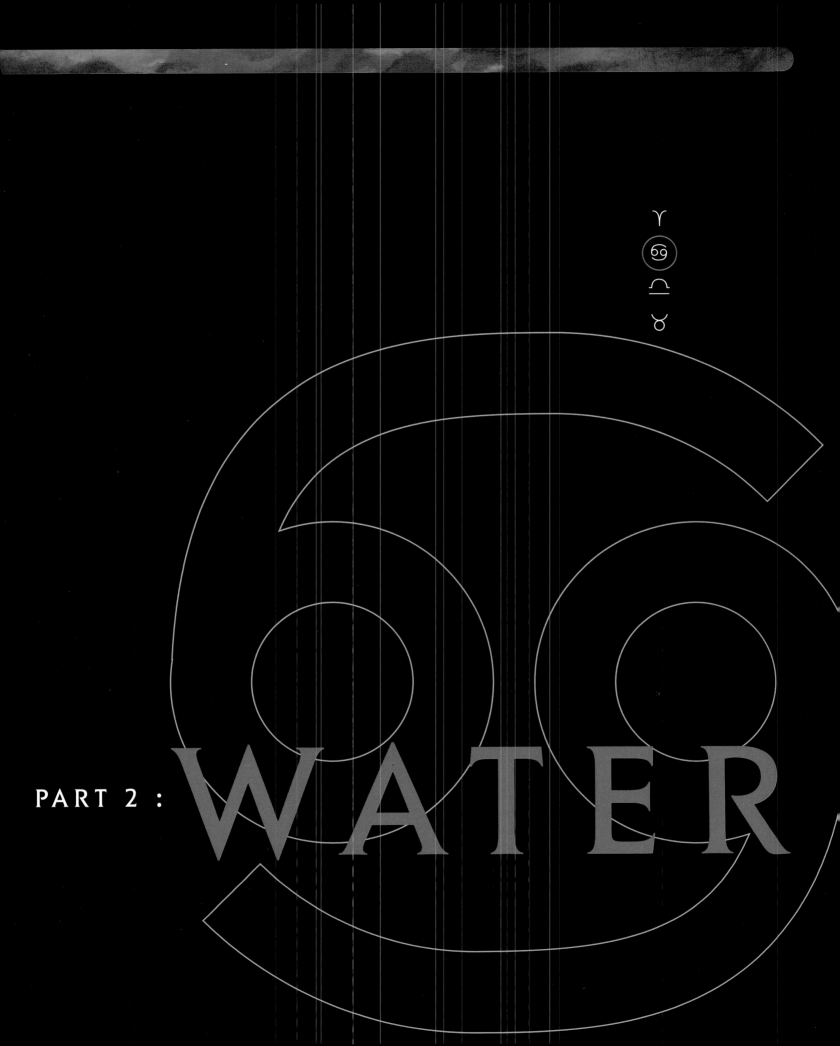

PART 2 : WATER

The sky is an angry purple womb, giving birth to torrent after cold, heavy torrent, turning the low buildings that surround us into a series of vague, gray shapes. Pulling my woven-fiber hood down more closely about my face, I try to escape the weight of the rain, if only for a moment. But there's no escape, no let up, no respite.

Crowds toss us like a tumultuous sea, everyone around us as wet and uncomfortable as we are. Small, shifty eyes flash in annoyance at us from beneath every kind of headgear imaginable—none of which proves very effectual against the relentless downpour.

My companion says something, but I can't understand him. The rain is drumming too loud on my skull. "I beg your pardon?" I yell.

He grabs me by the sleeve of my slick-jacket and pulls me down to his level. Then he bellows in my ear. "Los Angeles!"

"Los Angeles?" I reply wonderingly.

My companion's expression becomes one of disgust and he shakes his hooded head. "No, no, no . . . I say it's *scandalous*!"

A DRY DAY ON
FERENGI

A sheet of rain is driven into my already raw, stinging face. Wiping my eyes, I squint at him. "What is?" I ask.

"Seize her warms," my companion tells me.

"Seize her . . . ?" I echo helplessly.

Again, he screws up his face in frustration. "These reforms!" he yells at the top of his lungs.

I nod to show that I understand what he's said. I expect that he'll let go of my sleeve then, but he doesn't. Instead, he pulls me in the direction of a hovercar that's sliding to a halt just a few meters away.

Several other Ferengi rush after it as well, but my host and I get there first. I pay the driver an advance by slipping strips of latinum into a slot in the side of the vehicle.

Through a window, I can see the driver—who's nice and dry inside—counting and recounting the strips. Only after he's satisfied that he's received the proper sum does he slide open the door.

We pile in quickly, first my companion and then myself. A moment later, the door to the hovercar slides closed again, shutting out the hiss and bluster of the weather.

I wonder if I've lost my hearing. It's insanely quiet in here after the numbing din of the deluge outside. But not for long.

"Retirement benefits for the aged," says my host, a fellow named Quark. Pulling back his hood, he flicks a drop from one of his protuberant frontal lobes. "Wage subsidies for the poor. Health care for everyone." He looks as if he's swallowed something that went rancid weeks earlier. "I tell you, *hew-mon,* this is a dark time in the history of Ferenginar."

I look out the window in time to witness the arrival of another hovercar. Ferengi swarm around this one, too, elbowing and kicking one another to get to the slot where the latinum is inserted.

Rain sizzles around the conflict like a nest of hungry vipers. For a moment, the entire scene is whitewashed by a bolt of jagged lightning, followed closely by a *whip-crack* of thunder that threatens to make my heart stop. Then the crowd is folded into the gloom of the downpour again.

A dark time indeed, I tell myself.

On Earth, this would have been labeled a thousand-year storm, the kind of meteorological oddity one could tell one's grandchildren about. On Ferenginar, where the natives have 178 different words for rain and not a single word for "crisp," it's an everyday occurrence.

Of course, the rain is something the Ferengi have learned to cope with. Social reforms are a different story.

Ferenginar has been the galaxy's undisputed champion of capitalistic commerce. The reasons for this almost fanatical devotion are lost in the mists of ancient history, but that doesn't make it any less real.

Shortly after the Federation encountered the Ferengi Alliance in 2364, an Andorian diplomat was assigned the task of formal first contact. On his return to Federation space, he was asked what the Ferengi were like. He said, "It would be easier to separate a

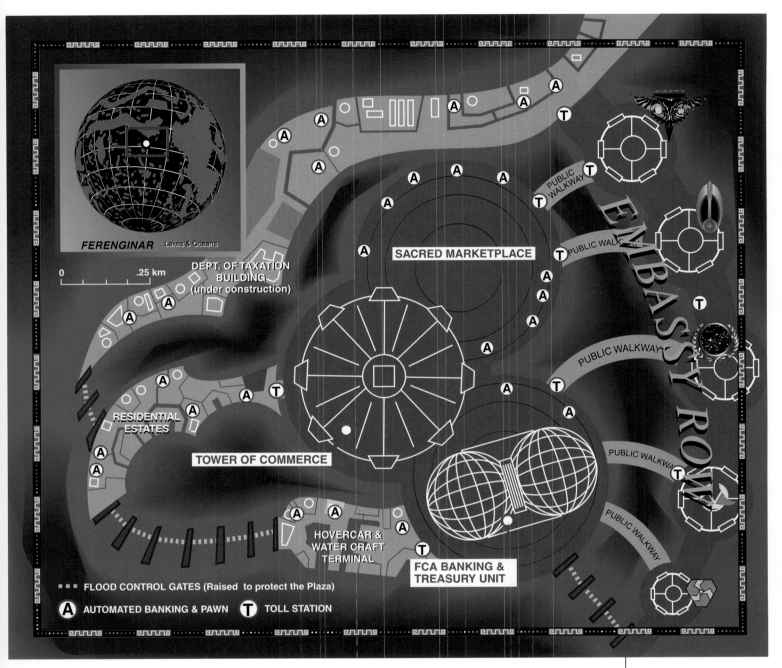

FERENGINAR Lakes & Oceans

0 .25 km

DEPT. OF TAXATION BUILDING (under construction)

SACRED MARKETPLACE

PUBLIC WALKWAY

PUBLIC WALKWAY

EMBASSY ROW

PUBLIC WALKWAY

RESIDENTIAL ESTATES

TOWER OF COMMERCE

PUBLIC WALKWAY

PUBLIC WALKWAY

HOVERCAR & WATER CRAFT TERMINAL

FCA BANKING & TREASURY UNIT

···· FLOOD CONTROL GATES (Raised to protect the Plaza)

Ⓐ AUTOMATED BANKING & PAWN   Ⓣ TOLL STATION

Vulcan from his logic than to pry a single slip of latinum from the hand of a dying Ferengi."

Subsequent ambassadors to Ferenginar have called their predecessor's assessment an understatement. They've found that Ferengi value the accumulation of profit above everything . . . even their own lives.

The contract is the cornerstone of Ferengi civilization. Any Ferengi found guilty of violating a bona fide agreement is liable to have his trading license revoked, in which case he becomes incapable of making profit.

And as the 18th Rule of Acquisition clearly states, "A Ferengi without profit is no Ferengi at all."

Quark is silent, caught up in some private thought. It's just as well. After the drone of thunder and the drumming of the downpour, I just want to sit quietly for a moment.

The capital city of the Ferengi Alliance. It was here the legend of the Ferengi eating their business partners started. A Triskelion refused to pay the toll on one of the bridges. He set across the low-lying swamp and was sucked into the muck and smothered. The toll keeper's report was garbled by a substandard universal translator into, "I ate him."

Quark, son of Keldar. He knows each and every one of the 285 Rules of Acquisition by heart. He spent the majority of his life earning profit off his homeworld, yet longs for the Ferenginar of his youth. He keeps reiterating that the changes are too much like "root beer."

Through the rain that sheets and splatters on our hover windows, I catch glimpses of immense, sky-prodding gray towers with spired tops and large-eared gargoyles spouting cascades of rainwater at every level.

The tallest edifice of all is the Tower of Commerce, a dark, articulated hive whose highest floors are lost in sooty billows of cloud. In addition to the largest and most striking collection of gargoyles around, the Tower is adorned with stately black columns, elaborate scrollwork, and dramatic friezes of pivotal moments in Ferengi mercantile history.

Its fortieth floor is home to the Ferengi Commerce Authority (FCA), whose name alone strikes terror into the hearts of Ferengi everywhere—and with good reason. The FCA monitors the business dealings of Ferengi on Ferenginar and elsewhere. Anyone believed to have violated a trade law is issued an ominous black scroll called a writ of accountability, which demands a detailed financial statement from the suspected wrongdoer.

If a Ferengi is found guilty of the charges, he can be fined or even, in extreme cases, barred from engaging in commerce with other Ferengi. And remember, "A Ferengi without profit . . ." Well, you know the rest.

At the Tower's base is the Sacred Marketplace, a vast, sprawling plaza full of shadowy, domed roofs, where traders of every conceivable kind of commodity haggle over the smallest nuance of even the most insignificant transaction.

Beyond the Tower and the Marketplace, the buildings begin to thin out and to change in character. The massive, almost sinister-looking office towers give way to smaller, more ornate structures with illuminated sculpture gardens and private *tongo* parlors—the estates of the wealthy, who have made their profits trading with off-world species.

I've heard that every one of these interstellar trading barons has a statuette of DaiMon Greko in his foyer. And well he should, considering it was Greko who opened up the spaceways to an eager Ferenginar.

Greko, son of Garjak, didn't show much promise as a child. He was boisterous, aggressive, blunt . . . not at all like his friends, who were miniature models of the conniving and calculating adults they would eventually grow up to be.

When the time came for Greko to leave his father's home, he didn't auction off his boyhood treasures to raise capital as was expected of a young Ferengi. Instead, he went to work on a Ridorian merchant ship, desiring above all else to see the wonders of the galaxy.

Or so it *seemed*.

In actuality, Greko was just as grasping and devious as any other Ferengi. It was just that he was a lot more ambitious. Instead of aiming to enrich only himself, he aimed to enrich his entire civilization.

And before long, he did just that. Though there are several versions of the story and none of them seems entirely dependable, this much is clear: Greko saved his captain's life when their vessel ran afoul of a Klingon bird-of-prey. As a reward, he was given a small fortune.

But that wasn't enough for him. In the master stroke of all Ferengi master strokes, Greko then used

Grand Nagus Oblatis is credited with the expression, "Get dry, young lobling!" By encouraging Ferengi to seek profit off-world he expanded Ferengi influence across the galaxy. After an hour on Ferenginar, most humanoid vistors agree: the pursuit of dryness, anything dry, is preferable to an existence in the constant rain.

that fortune to purchase an old, out-of-date warp drive from the normally hostile Breen.

To that point, few Ferengi had ever left Ferenginar, despite the 75th Rule of Acquisition ("Home is where the heart is, but the stars are made of latinum."). But once they realized what Greko had brought home, the rush for the stars began—and Greko became DaiMon Greko, a famous and extremely well-remunerated ship's captain.

Our hover passes a series of small, connected lakes that mirror the dark fury of the sky and the occasional burst of lightning. Apparently, 84 percent of Ferenginar is covered with such modest bodies of water.

After a while, Quark directs the hover driver to pull over in front of an interesting-looking mansion—one that's shaped like a Terran ant trying to stand up on its hindmost legs.

At Quark's suggestion, I pay the driver—who requests a substantial tip as well and refuses to let us out of his cab until he gets one. Quark's expression indicates that I should honor the request. I give the driver an extra slip of latinum, hear him mumble something about *hew-mons*, and see the door slide open.

Quark and I pull our hoods up over our heads. As we remove ourselves from the hover, the sky seems to disappear and we're hammered by the worst deluge yet. For a moment, I can't see more than an inch or two in front of me. It's as if I've gone blind as well as deaf. Then the rain lets up just enough for me to make out the mansion again.

"Come on," Quark yells in my ear. Then he grabs my arm and pulls me in the direction of the front door.

The door has a stylized Ferengi head made of some dark metal for a knocker. Quark uses it to rap twice. A moment later the door swings open and my companion pulls me inside.

We're greeted by a prosperous-looking Ferengi a bit shorter and a lot plumper than Quark. His name is Chek, I'm informed.

"Please to meet you," I tell our host. "I'm Sam Gooding of SubNet."

Understanding dawns in Chek's pudgy face. "Of course," he says appraisingly. "The *hew-mon* reporter."

I smile. "Exactly."

"Welcome to my home," says Chek. He hands me a padd. "Place your imprint on the legal waiver form and deposit your admission fee in the box by the umbrella stand. Remember, my house is my house."

"As are its contents," Quark replies accommodatingly.

"If you wish," Chek adds, "you may buy a buffet ticket for two slips of latinum per person. We're serving flaked blood fleas and baked *locar* beans this afternoon. Also, premium quality tube grubs."

"Fresh?" Quark asks shrewdly.

"And slimy," Chek tells him, "just the way you like them."

I catch a whiff of something vaguely fishy in the next room. Quark seems to have caught the same scent. He licks his lips.

"Don't forget the two hundred and fourteenth Rule of Acquisition," Chek says. "'Never begin a business negotiation on an empty stomach.'"

"This isn't a business negotiation," Quark points out.

"*Everything's* a business negotiation," Chek observes.

Quark considers the assertion. Then he says, "Point taken. Where do we purchase our tickets?"

Chek pumps his thumb over his shoulder. "See my wife in the corner there? She'll be glad to help you." As we move in the direction Chek's indicated, our host greets the next conspirator in line.

Chek's wife stands behind a small table beside the doorway into the next room. In accordance with the older Ferengi traditions, she's completely naked. I try not to stare as Quark and I approach her.

"Two tickets for the buffet," Quark tells her. He leans closer to me, grinning a sharp-toothed grin. "You can pay me back later, *hew-mon*. I think you'll find the rate of interest quite reasonable."

"Thanks," I say without much enthusiasm.

Chek's wife doesn't speak or even meet Quark's gaze. She merely holds her hand out until he gives her the latinum, then places it in a metal strongbox and tenders two tickets from the same box.

Until recently, all Ferengi females were kept housebound and uneducated, expected not only to prepare and serve their family's food but also to chew it for their husbands and male offspring. Grand Nagus Zek's first wave of reforms dramatically improved the status of females in most households.

Chek's is obviously not one of them.

For twenty-two years, Grand Nagus Zek was the brains of the Ferengi Alliance, opening up new territories for exploitation and exploring previously unexplored ways to make a profit. Then, seemingly without explanation, Zek began instituting a series of radical social reforms.

The first sign of his altered perspective was his declaration that females were to be treated like males in Ferengi society. In other words, they were to be allowed to wear clothes, get an education, speak to males who weren't family . . . even earn profit.

To the average Ferengi, this was nothing short of heresy. But Zek wasn't done yet. Not by a long shot.

Soon afterward, he came up with a collection of social welfare programs, including retirement benefits, wage subsidies, and worldwide health care. And to pay for it all, he called for a progressive income tax.

He then diluted his own power by creating a congress of economic advisors who had to ratify anything the grand nagus proposed. In other words, Zek began to steer Ferengi civilization in the direction of democracy.

Suddenly, monopolies were illegal. Corporations couldn't dump toxic waste in lakes and rivers anymore. Laborers were granted rights under the law. This was worse than heresy. It was absolute bedlam.

And who was responsible for this veritable upheaval in Ferengi philosophy? Who had single-handedly turned an entire starfaring civilization on its large, highly developed ear?

According to Quark, not Zek. He was the one who implemented the changes, certainly, but he wasn't the intelligence behind them. In fact, the mastermind

was none other than Quark's mother, Ishka, a forceful, enterprising female whom Quark's brother Rom still affectionately calls "Moogie."

That's the same Rom who recently succeeded Zek as grand nagus. And who do you suppose gave Zek *that* idea?

There are twelve Ferengi seated around a table in Chek's sumptuously appointed dining room, where portraits of his esteemed and well-dressed ancestors adorn the walls. (Prints can be obtained for a nominal donation, according to a small sign that appears below each of them.)

Chek's wife comes by and offers to chew my food for me, perhaps seeing that I haven't touched my plate of fleas, beans, and tube grubs. I hold a hand up to politely decline her suggestion, even less tempted by the prospect of a masticated grub than a whole one.

"Well, then," Chek announces in a stentorian voice as he pushes away his empty plate, "I hope you've all enjoyed your meal. Now let's get down to business, shall we?"

"Let's do that," Quark agrees.

"The question," says another Ferengi, "is what we're going to do about Zek's so-called reforms."

"And this idiot Rom that he's made grand nagus," someone else adds. He glances at Quark. "No offense intended."

"None taken," Quark grumbles.

"If things don't change," remarks another Ferengi, "we'll have a monetary collapse worse than the last one."

"Rampant inflation," Chek elaborates, unable to suppress a shudder of fear. "Currency devaluation."

"We can't let it happen," says the Ferengi on his right.

"We'll stand up to this Rom!" someone ventures animatedly. He looks around the table for a vote of confidence.

There are signs of hesitation all around the room. After all, Ferengi have historically been very reluctant to defy their nagus, no matter how big a problem he may pose. For a moment, it's not certain that the vote of confidence will come.

Then Quark speaks up, his eyes steely with resolve. "Dorl's right. We have to refuse to go along with the reforms that Zek instituted."

"Even though Rom's your brother?" Chek asks searchingly.

Quark frowns. "You know the 6th Rule of Acquisition—'never allow family to stand in the way of opportunity.'"

The dining room rings with cheers of approval. Quark's immediate neighbors slap him on the back in comradely fashion. Even Chek's ancestors seem pleased as they look down on the proceedings.

Apparently, Grand Nagus Rom is going to have to prove his mettle. He's going to have to show Ferenginar that he's got more going for him than his blood tie to Zek's life-partner.

Then again, these conspirators around Chek's table are going to be tested as well. They'll be risking their reputations, their profits, their sacred business licenses.

However, as the 62nd Rule of Acquisition clearly reminds us, "The riskier the road, the greater the profit."

Months earlier this house was the site of a summit between the factions, Grand Nagus Rom asked the Grand Nagus Emeritus Zek to preside. Quark reported that there was no movement. This left the traditionalists with one possible course—revolution.

DANULA II
THE FOOTFALLS OF TRADITION

There's a shallow furrow cut into the dry, cracked earth at my feet. It extends for a good thirty meters in either direction—enough to accommodate the fifty-five cadets who'll be testing their endurance this day.

A huge copper sun beats down on us from an immense purple-blue sky, stinging our flesh despite the salve we all wear, trying to sap our strength even before we've begun. In recognition of the difficult circumstances, Admiral Baker-Bowles wastes no time jogging over to one end of the shallow furrow and raising his arm.

I bend forward, plant my hands against the rough, dusty ground, and flex my knees as if nestling into starter's blocks. On either side of me, the other runners do the same. Then we eye the admiral again, trying to remain calm despite the inevitable heart-pounding rush of adrenaline. Baker-Bowles brings his arm down and we take off as one, a wave of cranberry and black washing across the colorless, barren land.

We won't finish that way, however. One of us will cross the finish line ahead of all the others. We just don't know who it will be yet.

The first Academy marathon celebrated the Khitomer Accords, the peace agreement between the Federation and the Klingon Empire that reshaped galactic politics eighty-two years ago. This marathon marks an even more important event—the end of our war with the Gamma Quadrant's Dominion, a war that claimed hundreds of thousands of Federation lives and threatened to make slaves of us had we lost.

When the first Academy Marathon was held following the historic Khitomer Peace Accords, the participants scarcely imagined what they'd set in motion. This piece, which hangs in the building at the Sharifi Rescue Site, was originally commissioned by the then commandant of the Academy to commemorate the first race. The other half hangs in the SportsCenter on the Academy grounds.

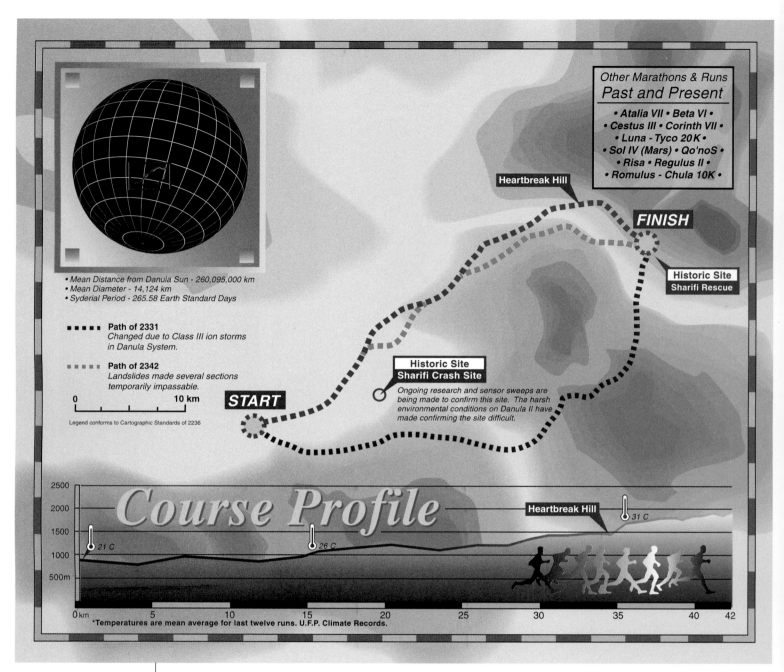

Other Marathons & Runs
Past and Present

• Atalia VII • Beta VI •
• Cestus III • Corinth VII •
• Luna - Tyco 20K •
• Sol IV (Mars) • Qo'noS •
• Risa • Regulus II •
• Romulus - Chula 10K •

Heartbreak Hill

FINISH

Historic Site
Sharifi Rescue

• Mean Distance from Danula Sun - 260,095,000 km
• Mean Diameter - 14,124 km
• Syderial Period - 265.58 Earth Standard Days

■■■■■ Path of 2331
Changed due to Class III ion storms
in Danula System.

■■■■■ Path of 2342
Landslides made several sections
temporarily impassable.

0 ————— 10 km

Legend conforms to Cartographic Standards of 2236

START

Historic Site
Sharifi Crash Site
Ongoing research and sensor sweeps are
being made to confirm this site. The harsh
environmental conditions on Danula II have
made confirming the site difficult.

Course Profile

Heartbreak Hill
31 C

2500
2000
1500
1000
500m

21 C   26 C

0 km   5   10   15   20   25   30   35   40   42
*Temperatures are mean average for last twelve runs. U.F.P. Climate Records.

Arrayed across the harsh environment of Danula II, the marathon course has changed several times over the years. The mean temperatures and the course profiles drive home the accomplishments of those who finish the race.

The race was—and still is—run on the parched plains and in the rocky hills of Danula II, a harsh world that hasn't supported life in at least a hundred thousand years. Why hold a marathon here? Tradition holds that the Academy commandant in 2293, a woman named Sharifi, had crash-landed on Danula II in her youth—and that she was so heartened by her ability to survive there, she wanted to pass the gift on to her cadets. Another account says she simply picked the place at random.

Needless to say, the Academy favors the first story.

Fourteen kilometers into the race, we're entering the highlands. I trudge up a long, barren slope, quadriceps burning, breath sawing painfully in my throat. Manute, a tall, lanky Bolian in the engineering curriculum, grunts and gasps alongside me.

The leaders, all formidable runners, are clustered in a pack seven or eight meters ahead of us. Everyone else is trailing us by twenty meters or more. Neither Manute nor I was expected to do this well at the outset, so we're rather pleased with ourselves.

However, there's something about being so near the vanguard that makes me greedy. I tell myself that if I can get to the top of the hill in good shape, I've got a chance to surprise some people. With a little luck, maybe I can even win.

Each competitor has been given a supply of half a dozen forced-release electrolyte capsules, which we carry in a small pouch attached to our left arms. I open the pouch, take out a capsule and swallow it. As the stuff washes through me, feeding my starved tissues, I feel invigorated. My legs don't hurt so much anymore either.

After a while, I realize that Manute has dropped back a few meters. I'm surprised. I don't remember him slowing down and I can't imagine that I've sped up. Refocusing my attention on the pack ahead of me, I try to ignore the heat and the dust and press on.

Over the years, the Academy marathon has generated tales of courage and perseverance in the face of adversity. None of them is more stirring than the famous finish of 2323.

There were four favorites in that race, it seems: Fergus McLeod, the winner of Earth's Boston Marathon in the sixteen-and-under category; Reggic Sipanos, a scaly, bronze-skinned Tessma who had won a few

championships of his own; and a couple of grim, gray-maned Arkarians.

The four of them ran neck and neck from the start, each one pushing hard in an attempt to leave the others behind. The result was a faster pace than any of them had really intended.

At the halfway point, there was no one else in sight—which was a good thing from their point of view, because they were all starting to run a little ragged. But as the race wore on, a slender human began to gain on them.

At twenty-five kilometers, they still had a hundred meters on him. At thirty kilometers, their lead wasn't much more than seventy meters.

But none of the front runners could believe the upstart was really a threat. For one thing, he was a freshman, and no freshman had ever won the Academy marathon. For another, none of them had ever raced against him before. He was a complete unknown.

I see the thirty-kilometer beacon blazing a bright, fiery red in the distance—and I still haven't lost touch with the pack. The Bolian, on the other hand, has dropped out of sight behind a gravel-strewn hillside.

I've gone through four of my six electrolyte capsules—too many, probably, at this point in the race. After all, with the burnished sun climbing steadily in the sky, it's only going to get hotter. But if I hadn't used all four of those caps, I wouldn't have been able to keep up the pace.

My legs are starting to feel rubbery with fatigue.

Sometimes one kilometer more is one too many. Win or lose, however, every runner in the Academy Marathon knows they race into history.

Just for a moment, I think about how good it would feel to stop and rest. But I won't let myself do that. I go on.

say Picard was born to lead; others insist his character was forged that day on Danula II.

WHEN WE COMPETE WITH OUR EXPECTATIONS OF OURSELVES, MANY VICTORIES ARE POSSIBLE.

Back in 2323, the four favorites were still bunched together when they reached Heartbreak Hill, the last and easily the most grueling leg of the course. After competing for thirty-five hot, brutal kilometers, none of them was eager to tackle a twenty-five degree incline that climbs into the sun for three thousand meters.

However, they knew that the race would be won or lost on that dry, crumbling slope, so they gritted their teeth and kept going. The Arkarians, who were renowned for their endurance, were nonetheless the first to give ground. Then came the Tessma. McLeod was all alone, it seemed, as he headed for the crest of the hill.

But before he could reach it, he heard the scrape of approaching footsteps. Thinking that Sipanos or one of the Arkarians had gotten a second wind, McLeod looked back over his shoulder—and saw the unheralded freshman he had long ago written off. The man was gradually closing the gap.

McLeod lost in the last twenty meters. The first-year cadet who beat him was Jean-Luc Picard, who later made a name for himself as captain of the *Stargazer* and then the *Enterprise*-D and -E. Some

Though I'm down to my final electrolyte cap, I'm running easily on the flats between the thirty-four-kilometer marker and Heartbreak Hill. Better yet, the bunch ahead of me seems to be tiring.

This is my chance, I tell myself. If I can bear down and beat them on the Hill, the race could be mine. What's more, it would be the first time a Betazoid has won.

All along, I've refrained from plumbing the minds of my fellow runners. But as I slowly but surely close with the pack, I can't resist a quick probe of the dark, leathery skinned Mikulak in front of me.

I expect her morale to be at rock bottom, considering she's falling back farther with every stride. But the Mikulak isn't demoralized. In fact, she's almost buoyant.

Making my presence known to her telepathically, I ask her why she's so happy. She glances over her shoulder at me and answers in the same wordless language. *I have won*, she tells me.

Do you really believe you'll finish first? I ask her incredulously.

No, she replies. *But I have won nevertheless.*

When we compete with our expectations of ourselves, many victories are possible.

I hadn't looked at it that way before, but I see her point. I'm still pondering it a minute later as I pass her.

Unfortunately, she's the only leader I manage to overtake. I get close to the others with the help of my last electrolyte cap, but they hold me off. Then we climb the long gray slope of Heartbreak Hill and my body begins to betray me. My legs cramp painfully and I feel light-headed, and I have no other capsules to keep me going.

There aren't going to be any Jean-Luc Picards here today, I tell myself bitterly. The leaders gradually leave me in their dust. Before I reach the crest of the hill even the Mikulak has gone by me.

In the end, I stagger across the finish line in seventh place. But when I get there, stiff-legged as a newborn colt and feverishly dehydrated, I see the Mikulak waiting to greet me.

"Did you win?" she asks me. She sounds far away.

Did I? I think about it for a moment—think about what she told me earlier. By the time I reach a conclusion, my mouth is too dry to frame the words, so I answer her telepathically.

Yes, I tell her. *I believe I did.*

It surprises me that I feel that way, but I do. In fact, I reflect as I limp away with the Mikulak's arm around me, I hope Jean-Luc Picard felt this good the day he won the Academy marathon.

Starfleet goes into one of the Maquis bases in the Badlands

THE SPECTER OF JAMESTOWN
BADLAN

Prussura IV is a Class-M world, if only barely.

The vegetation around us is sparse—just a few scrawny, purple stalks and spiked brush plants growing out of cracks in the gray, rocky terrain. Outside our helmets, the air is thin and full of radioactive plasma particles; they whip about like deranged fireflies in a fierce, shrieking wind.

The sky is a pale, oxygen-poor orange this morning. It'll be an even fiercer, wilder orange tonight. But then, that's true of all the planets here in the Badlands—even the inhabitable ones.

Ten of us have beamed down to the planet's surface. Commander Jusko, Lieutenant Montgomery, seven security officers, and me—a reporter for the Starfleet News Service. We're all wearing white, Starfleet-issue containment suits and transparent helmets. Jusko and the others are carrying shiny, new phaser rifles.

Me? I've got a padd so I can take notes.

Originally, I was to have waited for the second wave before beaming down from the *U.S.S. Crockett.* That's the accepted practice, so people like me don't get in the way of the fleet's "tactical professionals." Then we ran an orbital sensor scan and got the read-ing we'd been warned about.

No indications of sentient life.

The region of space known as the Badlands stretches for a span of nearly five light-years at the near edge of the Cardassian Union. It contains two young stars, seventeen planets, forty-three moons, and a rather sizable asteroid belt.

That's not the surprising part. What's baffled scientists throughout the Federation is that these bodies exist in a cosmic pressure-cooker, a fiery slice of hell alive with enormous, funnel-shaped plasma storms that confuse even the most finely tuned sensor systems and swallow starships as if they were plankton.

Few of the conditions that predictably give rise to suns and other celestial bodies prevail in the Badlands. And yet, the presence of suns and other bodies there is undeniable. One even finds *life*, as evidenced by the Class–M rating given to no less than three of the Badlands' planets.

This has led to speculation that the region's plasma storms are a relatively recent occurrence, one that may have begun to rear its ugly head as little as half a million years ago. But this theory begs other questions: Under what conditions did the storms originate? Is their sphere of influence spreading? And is it possible the Federation's other systems will fall prey to the storms in time?

Of course, those who have used this region as a hiding place over the years couldn't care less about the origin of the plasma storms. All that concerns them is that the Badlands keep the authorities at arm's length—and in most cases, they do that wonderfully well.

Jusko cradles her rifle in one hand and points to something in the distance, her fingers looking thick and bulky in the suit's gauntlets. I follow her gesture and see a large, research colony–style dome nestled among some crags. It's maybe twenty meters high and fifty in diameter. Not by accident, it's the same gray color as the rocks.

"That's it," says Jusko, her voice sounding a little tinny as it comes to me over our helmet radios. "Let's go. But be careful."

It's good advice. If there aren't any life signs here, it's because the enemy managed to drop by before we did—and the Cardassians have been known to leave calling cards in the form of disruptor mines.

Activating my suit's built-in tricorder, I scan the jumbled terrain ahead of me. No mines, according to my wrist-readout. I move forward with the others, picking my way among the rocks.

Even without any Cardassian leftovers around, we make slow progress. Though our suits protect us against the planet's ambient radiation and give us oxygen to breathe, they can't keep us from breaking a leg.

It takes us several minutes to get to the dome. I notice there aren't any holes or blast marks to mar the curved, gray surface. Nothing to indicate a violent confrontation.

The door, which conforms to the outline of the structure, is wide open. Jusko sends an officer in to check it out. He scans the area for booby traps, then turns and gestures that's it all right to proceed. Satisfied, the commander waves us forward again.

When we approach the doorway, I'm in the middle of the pack. My wrist-readout tells me I'm about to pass through an electromagnetic field operating at Starfleet Regulatory Agency standard output—enough to keep the plasma motes from flying inside, but not enough to stop something with the mass and motive power of a human being.

There must be a low-level field projector still in operation, I tell myself. When I pass through it, I feel the slightest flicker of resistance. Then I'm inside, getting my first live look at a Maquis camp.

What I see sends a chill down my spine.

The Badlands have long been used as a haven by smugglers, mercenaries, and others seeking to elude the authorities. But as far as anyone can tell, the rebels known as the Maquis are the only ones who ever took up residence on a Badlands planet.

The Maquis movement came about as a direct result of the Treaty of 2370, which ceded a handful of Federation border worlds to the Cardassian Union and vice versa. A number of Federation citizens on the affected planets were horrified at the prospect of Cardassian rule, but didn't want to give up their ancestral homes.

Feeling abandoned by the Federation, they formed a secret paramilitary organization to undermine the Cardassians' hold on them. From 2370, this organiza-

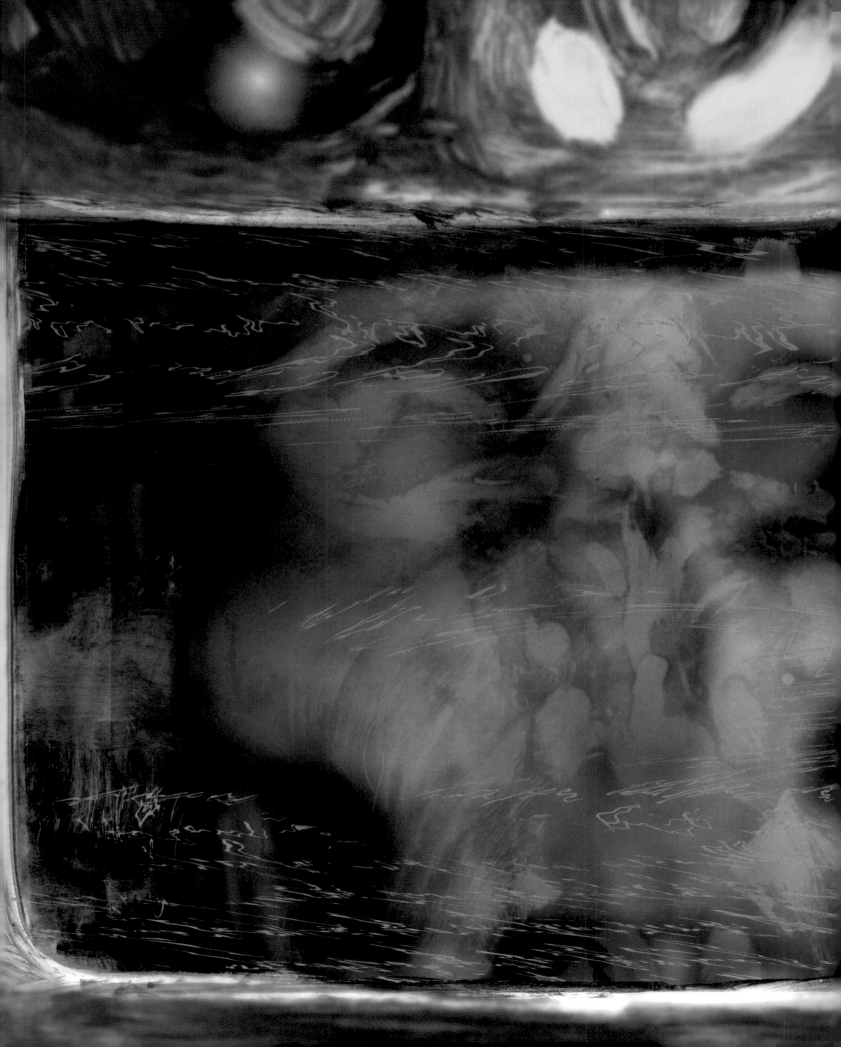

tion—dubbed the Maquis, after a French resistance movement during World War II—succeeded in making a rather large gadfly of itself.

On the other hand, I wasn't looking forward to a landscape full of barbecued corpses.

In the end, I went . . . and hoped for the best.

THE GOOD NEWS IS THAT THERE AREN'T ANY CORPSES. BUT THERE AREN'T ANY PEOPLE EITHER. NOT A SINGLE ONE, DEAD OR OTHERWISE.

However, in the long run, it didn't stand a chance. In 2373, the Dominion-backed Cardassians overran six Maquis strongholds in the Badlands, leaving little more than an army of burnt corpses.

When Federation intelligence got wind of the raid, they dispatched three starships to the Badlands to look for survivors. By some miracle, they found a few. But as far as anyone could tell, the Maquis movement had been brought to a stunning and hideous end.

Then one of the Maquis survivors, who had been sent to a penal colony on Earth, made a remark to a fellow prisoner about a seventh installation in the Badlands. He seemed to think the Cardassians might not have known about it. If so, the Federation still had a rebel nest to clean out—and a chance to get there before the enemy did.

Starfleet sent the *Crockett*, an *Excelsior*-class starship, into the Badlands to investigate. When SNS asked me if I wanted to go along, I was of two minds. On one hand, it was a chance to see Starfleet capture the last remaining stronghold of the infamous Maquis.

I remove my helmet and breathe decent air, which smells only slightly like rotten eggs. All around me, I see Jusko and the others remove their headgear as well.

In the center of the dome, there's a black plastic table with a couple of cups sitting on it and some chairs—an open conference area. The rest of the place is tightly packed with low, narrow beds and brown metal boxes, all of them illuminated by a collection of hanging light fixtures.

Everything looks like it's in good shape. There aren't any signs of violence. Approaching the conference table, I peer into the cups. They've got some kind of tea in them; it looks clear, as if it could still be consumed without risk of food poisoning.

The good news is that there aren't any corpses. But there aren't any people either. Not a single one, dead or otherwise.

Numbly, I approach a cluster of three beds and two boxes. There are pictures on top of a box. One of them shows me a family—a human mother with

I hear one of the younger officers mumbling something over his com link before he realizes it is open. I don't blame him. I try to think of something else, and suddenly from the recesses of my mind comes one word, "Jamestown." It was an ancient Earth settlement that was found deserted when a relief mission arrived. No trace of the survivors was ever found.

pale blonde hair, a human father with a receding hairline, and a little girl who borrows features from both of them. The other picture shows me a dark, frozen lake embraced by snowy, pine-flecked mountains.

Pulling open a drawer in the same box, I see clothes—the kind any family might accumulate. Men's clothes, women's clothes, children's clothes. Also, a small stuffed animal that resembles a Klingon *targ*, though it's so worn and beaten up it's hard to tell.

If the Maquis decided to leave, they would have taken that *targ* with them. But they didn't. I look around some more and notice bookpadds, personal grooming items, even some jewelry. I can't escape the impression that their owners will be back in a moment to pick them up.

Jusko's standing by another cluster of beds and boxes with her helmet tucked under her arm. She shakes her head, the muscles in her jaw rippling with dissatisfaction.

"Could they have left in a hurry?" I ask hopefully, my voice sounding much too loud in the confines of the dome.

Jusko's expression is neutral, but her eyes are full of sympathy. "I'd like to believe that," she says. "But I don't."

I sit down on one of the beds. It creaks beneath my weight. "So what did happen to these people?" I wonder out loud. "Did the Cardassians decide to take prisoners this time?"

Montgomery, a big man, picks up an empty animal cage. "Or did the Dominion give them a weapon that wipes out life without a trace?" he asks.

Jusko winces. "We may never know."

As a reporter, I hate those words. Unfortunately, it looks as though I'm going to have to live with them for a while.

I find consolation in only one thing—a feeling that this is one mystery Starfleet's going to want to solve.

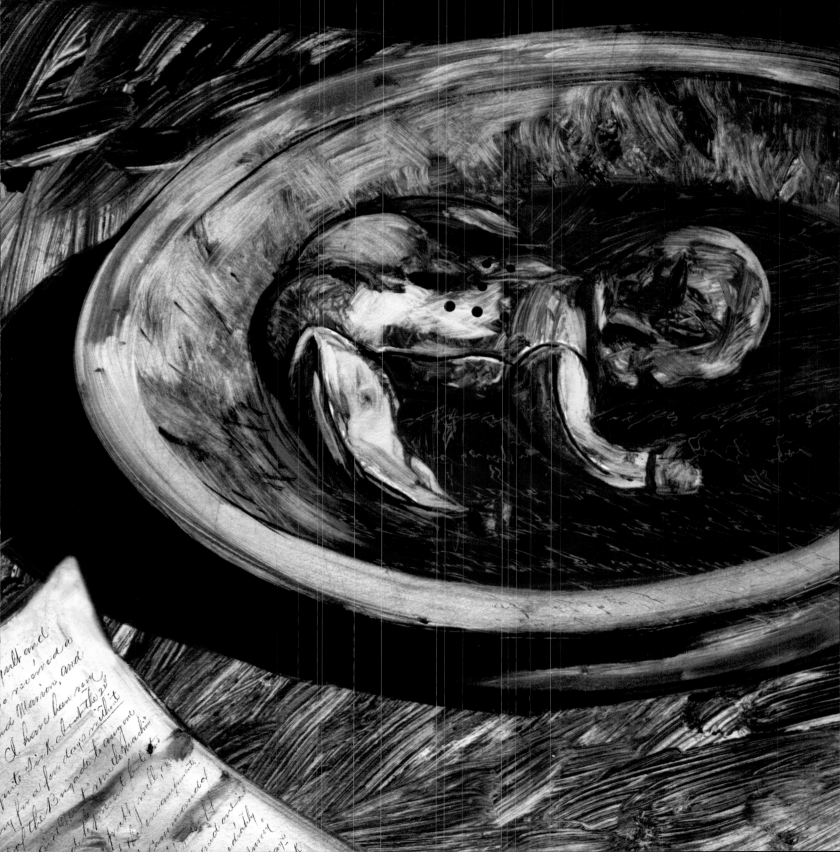

TRILL
AVERSION

The caves of Mak'ala stretch for kilometers under the surface of Trill—an elaborate network of small underground chambers illuminated only by light strips embedded in the stone walls.

Each chamber plays host to a pool of milky liquid which is connected to other pools of milky liquid. They couldn't be more packed with nutrients if our scientists had designed them that way.

This particular stone-walled chamber smells vaguely pungent in a rather pleasant way. The air is humid, the only sound the playful gurgling of water as it passes from one pool to the next. The currents reflect the light back at the cavern walls, creating spectacular effects.

I'm so mesmerized, I almost forget why I'm here. Reminding myself, I walk down a set of steps that have been carved deftly into the rock and seek out Timor, whose duties should have brought him to this point by now. There's no sign of him.

I would call out, but that would violate the sanctity of the caverns. So I wait patiently on a flat piece of rock and listen to the almost hypnotic music of the pools. Then something catches my eye.

Something is moving through the murky water, barely breaking the surface. No—there are two somethings.

The Guardian Timor's skill is evident, and he goes about his work with a quiet grace and a sense of delight. "Repetitive? Never! I am honored to be a Guardian!" he declares in an atypical outburst.

Suddenly, a spidery web of white lightnings passes between them.

Symbionts, I realize with a jolt of excitement. It's the first time I've ever seen one.

"They're sharing a joke," says a voice.

Whirling, I see a man with sleek, black hair and a long gray tunic. His eyes are protuberant, his nose long and thin, and his skin is as pale as a bottom-fish's belly.

> # ONLY ONE IN A THOUSAND TRILL CAN BECOME AN INITIATE . . . AND ONLY ONE INITIATE IN TEN WILL ULTIMATELY BE TRUSTED WITH A SYMBIONT.

"Timor?" I venture.

With a gentle, knowing expression, he jerks his head in the direction of the pool. "They don't have a very sophisticated sense of humor. But then, they haven't had many funny experiences yet."

I know the Guardians aren't used to visitors. "My name is Rantic Lan. I'm the new apprentice guardian."

Timor gazes at me appraisingly for a moment. "So you are," he says at last, his voice strangely devoid of inflection.

Retreating to a metal pedestal full of equipment, he removes a device with a long, cylinder projecting from it. Then he moves to the side of a pool, kneels, and activates it. A beam of light pierces the milky liquid.

Timor is testing several aspects of the pool water: ion concentration, temperature, viscosity. Everything has got to be just right. When he checks his gauges, he looks satisfied.

"Can I help?" I ask.

Timor looks up at me. "I suppose you'll have to, eventually. But not yet," he says.

Then he gets up, returns the device with the long cylinder to the metal pedestal and removes another one. As he moves to the next pool, I follow him, trying my best to be unobtrusive.

"You want to hear a story?" he asks without turning around.

I nod. "If you wish to tell me one."

"You really don't have a choice," Timor tells me matter-of-factly. "All apprentices have to hear it. It's part of your education."

"What's it about?" I inquire.

"It's about Aylim," he says.

"Aylim?" I echo, and the chamber echoes it again. But Timor doesn't answer. At least, not right away.

No one knows how, when, or why the first joining of Trill and symbiont came about. Some speculate that the symbionts reached out to us with their minds and compelled us to take them into our bodies. Others believe we were once one species and somehow grew apart. And still others say the symbionts are alien to this world—that they arrived from the void in prehistoric times.

There's no evidence to support any of these theories. On the other hand, there's no evidence to refute them either.

What we do know is that the symbionts are vermiform entities with a high degree of intelligence and an enormously long life span. In their natural state, they're sightless—not much of a disadvantage in a subterranean environment—but capable of propelling themselves through their underground pools and communicating via electrical discharges.

When they're sufficiently mature, the symbionts are implanted into the abdominal pockets of humanoid Trill hosts. The symbiont's intelligence is the dominant personality in the joined life-form, though the personality of the current and previous hosts are reflected as well.

Once joined, host and symbiont become mutually interdependent. After ninety-three hours, the host can no longer survive without the symbiont.

When it works, the relationship is beneficial to both parties. The symbiont derives sustenance and mobility from the host, while the host is allowed to experience the symbiont's remarkable intellect. What's more, where a symbiont has had previous hosts, its current host gains access to their memories.

For a joined Trill, nothing is more important than protecting the life of the symbiont—even at the expense of the host's life.

I follow Timor from cavern to cavern, watching silently and respectfully as he performs his duties. He appears to have forgotten about me, but I know that's not the case.

Finally, he speaks as he kneels by the side of a pool, ripples of rainbow light reflected on his face like living tattoos. "Aylim was a Guardian," he says, filling a vial with water from the pool and holding it up to the light of a strip. "He lived and worked in these caverns a thousand years ago . . . or so the story goes."

His eyes narrow as he appraises the contents of the vial. Then he empties the water back into the pool and gets up. He looks at me for a moment, his skin looking almost luminescent.

"How old are you?" he asks.

"I'm twenty-one," I tell him.

Timor draws a breath, then lets it out. "Come," he says. "We've got a lot of work to do."

And again, he moves on.

On Trill, there is no higher calling than the Joining. Only one in a thousand Trill can become an initiate, subject to the rigorous testing and evaluation process conducted by the Trill Symbiosis Commission, and only one initiate in ten will ultimately be trusted with a symbiont.

The Guardians—of which Timor is one—don't have to suffer through such a painstaking initiation process. However, they too enjoy a close relationship with the symbionts, giving up the pleasures of the world to live in the caves of Mak'ala and devote their lives to the symbionts' care.

Trill is dotted with deep, naturally heated pools. Theories abound as to what drove the first Trill to the deep underground caverns that are the home to the symbionts. Recent archaeological digs have pointed to some kind of planet-wide catastrophe, but there is still no definitive answer.

This involves more than just testing the water in the pools. Over time, the Guardians develop a rapport with the symbionts so they can know which ones are ready to be joined.

In fact, it's said that they know more about the symbionts than anyone—even the Trill with whom they're joined. If the tales are true, a Guardian can identify a symbiont just by gazing at its host.

It's mysteries like these that have drawn me to the caves the way a *silikh* fly is drawn to a flame.

Seeing how lovingly Timor follows the movements of the half-submerged symbionts, I feel a pang of longing myself. I want to know the pool-dwellers as he does. I want to serve them as he serves them.

"Why do you want to become a Guardian?" he asks me.

"I want to be close to the symbionts," I tell him.

"Why do you want to be close to them?" he prods.

I sigh. "I wanted to be joined, but that wasn't possible. My isoboramine levels were inconsistent."

"Being a Guardian isn't the same as being joined," Timor points out. "In many ways, it's like watching a celebration from a distance. You want to take part like everyone else, but you can't."

"I think I can manage that," I reply.

He looks at me for a while. Symbionts swim past, making ripples in the pool beside us. In the distance, a flicker of lightning dispels the darkness and then subsides.

"Aylim was only here a little while," Timor tells me, "a cycle shy of a solar year, when the tragedy took place." He says this as if we were speaking of Aylim all along.

"The tragedy?" I say.

Timor nods. "At the time, his record was spotless. Everyone agreed that he had the makings of a wonderful Guardian. He was diligent, intuitive, full of affection for the symbionts and his fellow Guardians as well. Then Marh swam downstream to one of the pools he was caring for."

"Marh was . . . a symbiont?" I guess.

"Yes," says Timor. "But it wasn't like the other symbionts. It was a rarity—a symbiont unfit for joining. We only see its like every hundred years or so."

A rarity indeed, I tell myself. "What was wrong with it?" I wonder aloud.

"Its biochemistry was such that it would have rejected its host like an organ from an incompatible donor." Timor gazes into the milky depths of the pool. "Aylim was very sad. After all, he knew what Marh was going to miss. He knew how limited its life experiences would be. And yet, there was nothing he could do about it."

I see a flicker of biochemical lightning illuminate an even more distant part of the cavern. I'm glad that these symbionts aren't flawed the way Marh was. I'm glad they'll all have hosts one day.

"We all grow close to the symbionts," Timor says. "So no one was surprised when Aylim grew close with Marh. Then, one day after last meal, one of the other Guardians found Aylim in the pool." A somber

pause. "He was trying to join with Marh."

I find that my mouth has fallen open and I close it. Joining is a delicate process, and not without its dangers even under the most carefully controlled conditions. As a former candidate, I know that all too well.

"How could he . . . ?" I stammer.

> "AYLIM WAS VERY SAD . . . HE KNEW WHAT MARH WAS GOING TO MISS . . . AND YET, THERE WAS NOTHING HE COULD DO ABOUT IT."

Timor continues to stare into the pool. "Aylim felt so badly for Marh, he couldn't accept Marh's inability to join. He convinced himself that it was all a mistake." Timor turns to me. "Otherwise, he would never even have considered anything so outrageous."

For a moment or two, the only sound is the gurgling of the water. Even the symbionts are still, as if they too are amazed.

"What happened to them?" I ask at last.

Timor's eyes go hard and glassy. "Aylim was unable to endure the strain of rejection. There was nothing one could do but drag his corpse from the pool."

I wince at the image. "And Marh?"

Lightning dances across the surface of the pool in front of us. It's as if the symbionts in the milky water have heard and understood us—though of course, that's impossible.

"Physically, Marh was unharmed. However, its contact with Aylim, no matter how brief, scarred it mentally. It was never happy again—not after it had received a taste of what it's like to be joined."

The horror on Timor's face tells me he's trying to imagine what that would be like. I try to imagine it, too.

"What Aylim did was an aberration," Timor says. "It has never been repeated. And as long as we have Aylim to hold up as an example, we need never mourn another Guardian."

I swallow hard. "I understand," I respond.

Timor goes on in a heartfelt tone. "But for all his foolishness, we must not condemn Aylim. What he did, he did out of—"

"Concern for the symbiont," I blurt out, wishing to show him how well I comprehend Aylim's plight.

Timor smiles wistfully at me, his face dappled with reflected light. "No, Rantic Lan. Not out of concern. Out of *love*."

PART 3 : AIR

AN ENIGMA WRAPPED IN A PUZZLE
GUARDIAN
OF FOREVER

Their names are Dulmer and Lucsly. They work for the Federation's Department of Temporal Investigations. Even here on the surface of a barren planet where the air smells like rust, they wear dark, tailored suits.

Although the Guardian was discovered in 2267, Starfleet has only recently handed over responsibility of maintaining the site to the Office of Temporal Investigations. Long considered a "backwater outpost for recruits with no future," the new site managers, Dulmer and Lucsly, insist that they are too busy to comment.

Dulmer is short and spare with blunt features, thinning blond hair, and a perpetual scowl. He looks suspicious of everything. Lucsly is tall and dour, with a long face, dark hair combed back off his forehead, and a narrow, aristocratic nose. He has a padd in his hand.

"You're the reporter," Dulmer notes, squinting as the wind blows some sparkling mineral dust at him.

I do my best to look friendly. "That's right."

Before I can offer the man my hand, he heads for a cleft in the jumble of blue and purple crags that surrounds us. Lucsly waits until I fall in behind Dulmer. Then he follows as well.

"I hope you don't take this lightly," he says in a cultured voice.

I glance at him over my shoulder. "As a matter of fact, I don't."

"Good," says Lucsly, jotting something down on his padd. "We hate it when people take temporal phenomena lightly."

A moment later, we emerge from the rocky cleft and I see a sprawling array of ancient gray ruins. Broken columns, cracked arches, and time-worn blocks of stone cover the landscape all the way to the horizon.

In the middle of them, dominating them, stands a rough-hewn, irregularly shaped stone doughnut about three meters in diameter. Even without a tricorder, I can feel it pulsating with power . . . just the way I was told I would.

I turn to Dulmer. "The Guardian?"

"The Guardian," he confirms gravely.

Five years ago, when the Federation Council declassified them, I began an in-depth study of the logs of Captain James T. Kirk.

Kirk, who commanded the *U.S.S. Enterprise* on and off for nearly thirty years in the latter half of the twenty-third century, was one of my boyhood heroes. I couldn't wait to hear his adventures on other worlds described in his own words.

To my disappointment, I found that the logs made available to me had some holes in them. When I inquired, I was told that they had been purged of "security-sensitive" data. What was left was interesting, certainly, but hardly the deep insight into Kirk that I was looking for.

It occurred to me that Kirk's colleagues might have had a few interesting things to say about him. I examined their logs as well, but ran into the same problem—gaps in the really good stuff. Again, I was told that information had been withheld for the sake of Federation security.

Could I petition to have this data restored? I asked. The council told me I could ask for certain pieces of information to be declassified—but my success would depend on the specificity of my request.

Typical bureaucratic mumbo-jumbo, I thought. Before I could be allowed to learn about something, I would have to have some knowledge of it.

Nonetheless, I delved into the logs all over again, Kirk's as well as his officers', hoping for a shred of information that would give me an excuse to ask for more. To my surprise and delight, I found something.

It wasn't much—just a passing reference in one of Hikaru Sulu's personal logs. As a botany enthusiast, he liked to come up with strange and exotic names for the hybrids he created.

When Sulu crossbred a Klingon fireblossom with a Benzite dream-of-darkness, he called it an "Edith Keeler"—and gave it to his captain as a gift. His hope, he said, was that it would give Kirk "some comfort."

The Guardian seems to be waiting for something. For me, I think.

"Can I speak to it?" I ask Dulmer, removing my padd from the pocket of my jacket.

The blond man squints at me. "That was the deal under the Freedom of Information Act." Nonetheless, he doesn't look very happy about it.

I walk up to the stone portal, through which I can see what looks like a Greek temple on a distant hill, and speak over the hooting of the wind. I feel strange. I've never interviewed a hunk of rock before.

On the other hand, I'm not insensible to the magnitude of the opportunity. I can only imagine the euphoria ancient archaeologists might have experienced if they could have conversed with the bones they unearthed.

"What are you?" I ask the Guardian.

"I am the Guardian of Forever," the portal replies in a deep, remarkably resonant voice. As it answers, it glows with a weird silver light.

Like a kid who's just been transported for the first time, I can't help smiling a little. "Are you a machine?" I ask. "Or a living being?"

"I am both and neither," the Guardian informs me.

"What's your objective?" I ask.

"I am my own beginning, my own ending," it says.

That's interesting. "Do you mean you created yourself?" I ask the Guardian. "Or that, in time, you'll come to destroy yourself? Or maybe both?"

There's a brief pause. "I am incapable of answering in terms your primitive mind can grasp."

Dulmer and Lucsly look vaguely satisfied at the difficulty I'm having. But then, they don't know where I'm going in my conversation with the Guardian.

Taking careful notes on my padd, I plunge on.

Edith Keeler.

As I said, I had gone over Kirk's logs pretty thoroughly. I knew the name of every crewperson who ever served under him—and none of them were named Edith Keeler.

A friend, then? A lover? A relative? These were all possibilities. The only way to find out for sure was to search the press corps database.

To my surprise, there weren't any Edith Keelers in the twenty-third century. The last one, it seemed, was a "social worker" who lived way back in 1930, long before Earth launched its first space probe. She had died in a car accident.

What kind of connection could there have been between a twentieth-century woman and Captain Kirk? Or was Sulu referring to an entirely different Edith Keeler, one who was somehow not listed in the database?

I could have taken the name to the Federation Council, but I didn't think this was the kind of puzzle they could solve. So I contacted one of the few people alive who might have known what Sulu meant.

A short time later, I found myself speaking across a subspace link with the elderly but keen-eyed Admiral Leonard McCoy.

Dust swirls around my feet. "I would like to see the past of the planet Earth," I tell the Guardian.

"Behold," it says.

A moment later, the opening in the rock mists over and I see images begin to flitter behind it. There's a musty smell in the air, though there's precious little water in this planet's atmosphere. As the mist clears, the images become more vivid, more lifelike.

I see slender, bronze-skinned men waging war with clumsy iron swords and iron-plated shields. I see scantily clad slaves hauling blocks of stone up wooden ramps to build great pyramids. I see senators in robes and sandals arguing the fate of their empire in a proud, open forum.

The images change so quickly, I can't absorb much in the way of details. I could ask the Guardian to slow down, but I know it won't accommodate me.

Out of the corner of my eye, I can see Dulmer and Lucsly watching, ready to pounce in case I decide to take advantage of what the Guardian is offering me—participatory access to the past. But I just stand there, taking in the wonder of it.

McCoy knew who Edith Keeler was. He knew only too well.

With a healthy disregard for red tape, he told me how the *Enterprise* encountered a pattern of time displacement waves and traced it to the Guardian. He also told me how he, the ship's doctor, accidentally injected himself with a hypospray full of cordrazine. Caught up in a paranoid delusion, he beamed himself down to the Guardian's planet.

Kirk and a security team followed—and found the Guardian. It was Spock, Kirk's first officer, who determined that the thing was a million years old. It was Spock too who recognized the Guardian for what it was—a means of accessing other periods in time.

In the meantime, the cordrazine-crazed McCoy leaped through the Guardian into Earth's past—more specifically, Earth in the 1930s, where he saved the life of one Edith Keeler.

Unfortunately, that single act twisted history as we know it, obliterating the events that led to the creation of the Federation and the existence of a *Starship Enterprise*. Kirk and his landing party found

Its function is every bit as puzzling as its form; the sentient time portal that calls itself the Guardian of Forever stands alone amidst the ruins of a forgotten civilization. For a glimmer of a moment it replays a fragment of Earth's history — the first steps *Homo sapiens* took upon another world, and toward the exploration of the stars.

themselves stranded in a pocket of timelessness, with no past and no future.

In an attempt to set things right, Kirk and Spock went after McCoy. Kirk eventually restored the timeline by preventing the doctor from rescuing Keeler—but only after the captain had fallen in love with the woman.

Spitting out Kirk, Spock, and McCoy, the Guardian assured them that their place in time was secure again. But it wasn't finished. It had a proposition. "Many such journeys are possible," it informed Kirk. "Let me be your gateway."

The captain wisely declined the offer, according to McCoy's account. But the fact that it was made at all raised some questions in my mind.

Armed with something specific to petition for, I went to the Federation Council. To my delight, they granted my request for an interview with the Guardian.

"I AM THE GUARDIAN OF FOREVER," IT INSISTS.

Gazing into the Guardian's maw, I watch the fiery launch of the Apollo XI spacecraft that was the first to deposit human life on Earth's moon.

A second later, in the rice paddies of Southeast Asia, the armies of Khan Noonien Singh exchange bursts of gunfire with the forces of another genetic superman. By the harsh light of bonfires, riots tear apart a Sanctuary District in San Francisco. Vulcans

emerging from an interstellar craft draw a motley crowd of post-World War III humans.

It all passes before my eyes. Year after year, decade after decade, century after century.

Interestingly, the Guardian isn't consistently showing me the events I expect to see—the events you and I have come to think of as turning points in man's development. But I don't think it's displaying random occurrences either. It's just that its perspective is an alien one.

In any case, I haven't come here simply to put the Guardian through its paces. Hard as it is for me to believe, I have even bigger fish to fry. "Thank you," I tell the time portal, "but I'd like to ask another question."

The Guardian mists over again and the musty smell returns. A moment later, the historical images cease. "I am listening," the Guardian tells me with an unmistakable note of eagerness in its voice.

In the hundred years or more since Kirk's *Enterprise* discovered it, the Guardian must have been presented with a great many questions. It's good to know it isn't tired of answering them.

"Are you really a Guardian?" I ask.

"I am the Guardian of Forever," it says.

"What is it you guard?" I wonder aloud.

"I am the Guardian of Forever," it reiterates stubbornly.

I was afraid of this. But I'm not done yet. "How many times have you been accessed as a time portal?"

"Hundreds of times," the Guardian tells me.

"In the last century or—"

"That's classified," Dulmer snaps, stopping me short.

"Federation security supercedes the rights and

privileges of Federation citizens," Lucsly adds a bit too ominously for my taste. "Regulation twenty-one, section six, paragraph four."

I accept their position, having been warned in advance that I haven't got complete carte blanche here. Turning back to the Guardian, I say, "You've been accessed hundreds of times?"

"That is correct," it confirms.

"And on how many of these occasions has the timeline been altered?"

"All but six," the Guardian replies.

The answer isn't entirely unexpected, but hearing the words spoken out loud makes my knees weak. If the timeline's been altered that often . . .

"Exactly where are you going with this?" asks Dulmer, stepping forward. His steely eyes have narrowed to a fine point.

"Yes," Lucsly chimes in, "where?"

I shrug. "For someone who's supposed to be guarding something—a little thing called *forever*, in this case—the Guardian seems pretty free and easy with the thing it's guarding."

The DTI men exchange what appear to be meaningful glances. It's Lucsly who eventually responds, saying, "The Guardian's logic is beyond our understanding."

"No doubt, some of it is," I concede. "But it manages to communicate with us. That suggests we have a few things in common."

"What are you getting at?" Dulmer demands.

"Well," I say, "I've been thinking. On one hand, the Guardian must have been designed to protect the time-stream, or it wouldn't keep referring to itself as

a guardian. On the other hand, it invites us to violate the timestream every chance it gets."

"And?" Lucsly prods.

"And that's a contradiction," I tell him. "Unless, of course, the Guardian's here to preserve the time-stream by facilitating changes in it."

"Preserve it . . . by changing it?" Dulmer smiles, but there's no humor in it. "That doesn't make sense."

"Doesn't it?" I ask. "What if the timestream's under constant stress? And the only way it can keep from snapping in a big way is by snapping in little ways from time to time?"

"That's absurd," says Lucsly. But at the same time, he's writing something down on his padd.

"Are you finished?" asks Dulmer.

"In a moment," I tell him. Then I address the Guardian again. "Am I right? Are you preserving the time-stream by permitting it to change?"

"I am the Guardian of Forever," it insists.

But I'm beginning to understand now. "Of course you are."

"Time's up," says Dulmer in no uncertain terms.

As the planet's metallic dust blows around us, I nod. "If you say so," I tell the DTI agent.

After all, I've gotten what I came for. It occurs to me that if Kirk were still around, he might be proud of me.

At least, it makes me feel good to think so.

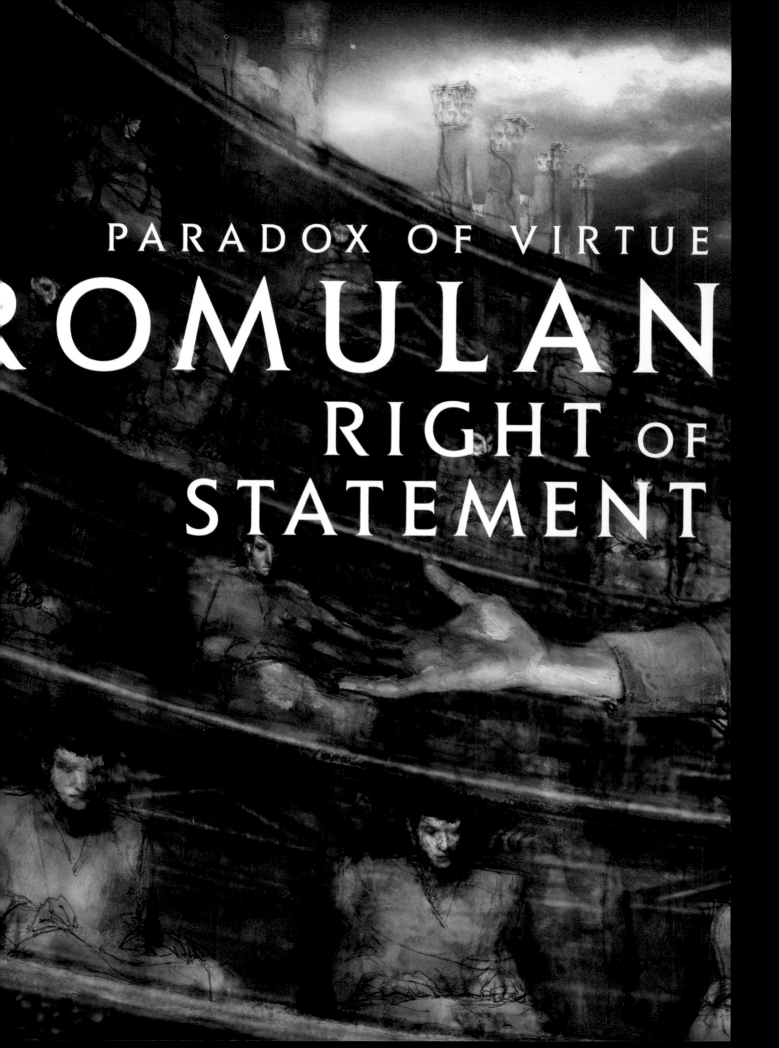

PARADOX OF VIRTUE

ROMULAN

RIGHT OF
STATEMENT

An open air amphitheater that seems to recall the glories of Earth's ancient Greece is the stage for J'Kor's "Right of Statement." Built on a heroic scale, its designers wanted the "…citizens to remember the soaring glories of Romulus."

J'Kor speaks, with the larger of his planet's two red-orange suns at his back, his dark-haired figure throwing a long shadow as it abides in the midst of solar fire.

His words ring out to the limits of the sunset-washed amphitheater, a rough-hewn granite structure about ten meters high and fifty in diameter, and are thrown back at him in a chorus of ghostly echoes. To my naked and unaided human ears, they sound like the lyrics to an especially passionate and plaintive love song.

It's spring here, the planting season. The air is redolent with the sweet, earthy smell of new life. All around us, seas of blue and yellow blossoms bow under the press of the evening storm winds. Clouds mounting in the east open like colossal scarlet roses against a slowly darkening sky.

For a moment longer, I resist using the universal translator in my borrowed communications badge, preferring to hear J'Kor's argument the way his judges hear it—in all its heartfelt beauty. Then, so as not to lose the sense of it, I reactivate the translator.

J'Kor, who no longer calls Romulus his home, speaks of his birth province there—a region of dark,

smoldering hills and sunset rivers, where the soil was fertile and the fields were bountiful. It's where he met his wife, he says. It's where they began their family.

His children were half-grown when some of his neighbors suggested that he go into politics. The praetor for their district had passed away and a replacement was needed. J'Kor reminded them that he had no experience with making laws. Neither had his predecessor, they noted.

So, J'Kor tells us, he went to the capital and represented them in the praetorate. And for a time, he did an excellent job. Everyone told him so. Through hard work and perseverance, he made his district's needs known and saw them met.

Years passed, says J'Kor. He grew in influence and prestige. He moved his family to the capital and married his daughters to wealthy men. He saw his wife inducted into an honored society.

"Life was good," he tells the fifty or so of his fellow Romulans who have gathered in the amphitheater to hear him out. "I accomplished great things. My honor shone like the sun."

That, he tells them, his wrinkled chin lifted in an attempt at dignity, is why it is so hard to accept the charges against him.

The Romulan Right of Statement is as old as Romulan civilization itself, or so I've been told by the handful of Romulans who've deigned to speak with me. Before there were cities on Romulus or Remus, before there were praetors or proconsuls, Romulans charged with a crime had

Unlike their stoic "cousins," the Vulcans, Romulans are driven by their passions. This has inspired a harsh moral code that guides that society, and a harsher penal code for even the most minor social infractions.

the opportunity to address the issue of their guilt or innocence.

Interestingly, there's no time limit placed on the Right of Statement. If the accused wishes to ramble for days and has the requisite fortitude, no one will attempt to stop him.

There are analogies to this custom in a hundred other cultures and civilizations, not to mention Starfleet jurisprudence. For instance, both the Celotti and the Igaaren give their citizens a worldwide telepathic forum whenever they feel they've been slandered. And on Okapu VII, the privilege of verbal defense is extended not only to an individual but to his clones as well—no matter how many of them there might be.

J'Kor frowns and falls silent—but only for a heartbeat. Then he goes on, speaking of terrible things.

A rumor swept the praetorate, he says. There were those who wished to see the Romulan and Vulcan peoples unified into the single species they were reputed to be. J'Kor, who had no such wish at the time, tried to distance himself from the rumors.

However, they eventually caught up with him. He was seized by the Tal Shiar, stripped of his title and his lands. His wife, he tells the assemblage with dark eyes painfully bright, was dragged from her house and killed. His daughters suffered the same fate.

J'Kor too would have been destroyed, he says,

"... WE'RE FAR FROM HOME. TRADITIONS MUST CAST A LONGER SHADOW HERE THAN THEY DID ON THE WORLD OF OUR BIRTH."

However, these are open societies, where a wide variety of personal freedoms are allowed to flourish. One doesn't expect to see a Right of Statement in a repressed and regimented culture, where the agents of the Tal Shiar—the Romulans' merciless secret police—seem poised to pounce on even the smallest transgression.

Nonetheless, a strain of individualism seems to have survived among the Romulans. An agrarian-style air of independence still motivates them, compelling them to speak their minds.

And they do.

but for the Reunification underground. Ironically, the movement that had caused his downfall became his salvation, and the people he had decried as traitors in the praetorate became his closest friends.

For more than a year, he says, he worked with the movement, helping to spirit Romulan defectors across the Neutral Zone to the Federation. And all the while, he mourned the loss of his wife and daughters, not a day going by when he didn't think of them. Then, finally, his cell was exposed and it became his turn to leave Romulus.

That, he says, is how he came to this M-class world and joined a growing community of Romulan expatriates. But there's more to J'Kor's story.

He had been living on this world, in this village, for nearly a year when the woman known as Ethara arrived. "I found her appealing," J'Kor tells the assemblage soberly. "I believed she found me appealing as well. And I had mourned my wife for a long time, you see. It was time, I convinced myself, for a new beginning after all my travails."

J'Kor turns to regard a severe-looking female seated in the third row of stone benches. His eyes grow regretful under the jutting ridge of his brow. "I did not know she was betrothed to another when I approached her in her garden. Otherwise, I would not have been so . . ." He hesitates, seeking the precise word to describe his crime. "Purposeful."

Finally, J'Kor falls silent and takes his seat in the first row—the only one allowed to do so. His neighbors—also his judges—mull over what he's told them as the sun vanishes in a pool of bloodred light and the first faint stars emerge in the heavens. The shadows fade.

By human standards, J'Kor's crime was little more than a lapse in manners. But to the Romulans, with their rigid social guidelines, it's a good deal more serious than that.

Of course, it's important to J'Kor that he not be found guilty. He hopes that his peers will understand the extenuating context in which he acted and have mercy on him. If they don't, he'll be ostracized from the community for a prescribed time—no small penalty.

But to the other Romulans in this community of exiles, J'Kor's guilt and innocence pale beside the fact that he exercised his Right of Statement. After all, as one of his judges told me earlier, "We're far from home. Traditions must cast a longer shadow here than they did on the world of our birth."

The pilgrim's path. Young and old consider walking in the path of the Emissary to be akin to taking a step closer to the Prophets. The devoted fill the roads. They are a respectful, joyous throng.

BAJOR

A WALK IN THE PATH
OF THE EMISSARY

They've been praying at the edge of the river in their fluttering orange robes for weeks now, their words mingling with the whispers that emerge from its blue depths.

There are more than a hundred of them in all. They spend part of the day chanting the ancient atonal hymns, a few moments consuming the bread and spiced *klemmen* and water they've brought with them, and the rest in contemplation of the valley's opposite slope.

To the untutored eye, there's nothing unusual about the vista, nothing to set it apart from all the other shaggy, green hillsides in this very fertile part of Bajor's Kendra Province. It has a few bulges of light-gray rock, but they're certainly common enough. And the scrawny *timpok* tree growing out of a crack in an outcropping is hardly what one would call remarkable.

But to the hundred and more Bajorans who have planted themselves here in awe and devotion, those twelve hecapates of sloping land are nothing short of sacred . . . nothing short of miraculous. After all, this is the land the Emissary purchased before he joined the Prophets in the Celestial Temple.

And when he comes back, or so the story goes, the Emissary plans to live out his days there.

"More *hasperat*?" asks my guide, a herdsman named Geneb who's singularly unimpressed by all the orange robes. He holds out another piece for me in a paper wrapper.

I hold up my hand. "No," I say a bit too quickly, "thank you."

The truth is that my mouth still smarts from my previous bite of *hasperat*, which tastes like fire in a pastry shell. Besides, I'm eager for us to be on our way. I say so.

Geneb shrugs his bony shoulders. "Then let's go," he tells me, and leads the way downriver.

It was only a few months ago, at the height of the war with the Dominion, that Captain Benjamin Sisko attended a tactical conference in the heart of Rakantha Province.

Before he returned to Deep Space 9, which he commanded by agreement of the Federation and the Bajoran Provisional Government, a vedek named Oram invited him to take a side trip. Oram's monastery in Kendra Province was several thousand years old and he thought Sisko might like to see it. Whether out of courtesy or curiosity, the captain accepted.

They took a transport over the twisting spine of the lush Mennekaren Mountain Range, which divides hilly Kendra from the flat farmlands of Rakantha. Vedek Oram spoke of the furnishings in his monastery, which were even older than the building itself, and Sisko—who had a great respect for ancient things—seemed to enjoy the conversation.

But as they crossed the Yolja River Valley, with the setting sun bathing it in a ruddy light, the captain found he couldn't take his eyes off the place. It was as if his heart had been hidden from him all his life and he had only at that moment caught sight of it.

Sisko saw himself building a house in this valley

after the war was over. He saw himself being happy there, at peace with himself. It was more than an aspiration. It was like a vision.

Seeing how taken Sisko was with the site, Vedek Oram asked the transport pilot to land and let them out. Then, as the sky flamed with a magnificent sunset, he began walking alongside the river.

"Where are you going?" Sisko asked, well aware that it would be night soon, and that it got cold at this altitude even in summer.

"You'll see when we get there," the vedek told him.

A few kilometers' walk from the crowd of orange-robed worshippers, at a picturesque bend in the Yolja, Geneb and I come to a small inn with white stucco walls and a slanted wooden roof. According to my guide, it's called The Emissary.

It seems like a grandiose name for so simple a place. Then Geneb tells me it's only been called The Emissary since Sisko and Vedek Oram spent the night there. Before that, it was called River House.

Geneb asks me if I want to get a drink there— some spiced tea perhaps. I decline, though I can smell its pungent aroma beckoning from an open window. After all, there's a lot more to see.

We continue our trek alongside the river. The ground underfoot is sandy sometimes and covered with pebbles at other times. The pebbles make for slower going, but that's all right. After all, Sisko and his friend the vedek had to put up with the same problem after they left the inn.

Before long, the steep, green slopes of the valley fall away on either side of us and the Yolja flows a little more slowly. Its voice changes too, becoming more of a gurgle than a whisper. I inhale the sharp scent of *nipujan* bushes, which thrive at some of the middle altitudes, though I don't see any—at least, not yet.

> HE SAW HIMSELF BEING HAPPY THERE, AT PEACE WITH HIMSELF. IT WAS MORE THAN AN ASPIRATION. IT WAS LIKE A VISION.

As the sun climbs higher into the blue expanse of the sky, my throat begins to feel a little parched, and I wish I'd stopped to have some tea as Geneb suggested. Of course, I can easily dip my hands into the river and satisfy my thirst that way, but I prefer to pursue another course.

Then I see it, up ahead in the emerald-green hills to my right—a squarish pile of pale, bleached rocks with the overgrown ruins of a red-stone village behind it. The pile of rocks has a wooden bar suspended above it on two upright pieces of wood. As I get closer, I see that there's a roughly made *binjana* rope tied around the bar.

Geneb points it out, but with a wave I dismiss the need for him to do so. I've seen enough pictures of the well to recognize it. It was the same one Captain Sisko and Vedek Oram encountered months earlier when they made this same pilgrimage.

"You know the story?" Geneb asks me as we leave the riverside to approach the well. "The story of the well?"

"I do," I assure him. "Before they left Bajor in 2369, the Cardassians injected chemical pollutants into farmlands, lakes, reservoirs, and even seemingly insignificant country wells like this one. But when Sisko and the vedek arrived here, they were thirsty."

Geneb nods as we reach the well. "Then a herder, like myself, saw them from a distance and recognized Oram as a vedek. Approaching the travelers, he asked if he could bring them some water from the river, which had spilled from the mountains and was therefore untainted."

"But Captain Sisko declined," I say. "He told the herder that he had gone toe to toe with the Jem'Hadar—and that he wasn't about to back off from the possibility of a little Cardassian poison."

I run my hands over the smooth, worn stones of the well, then lean forward and peer down into the darkness. I don't see much, but I feel and hear a breath of cool, moist air. Taking hold of the rope and picking it up a bit, I test the weight on the end of it.

It's manageable, even for someone like me who doesn't leave his desk much. I begin pulling the rope and the weight up out of the well. After a while, I get to the end and see what I've been hoisting—a wooden bucket not much bigger than my fist.

It's full of cool, clear water. I take a sip and feel it wash through me. In my memory, no beverage has ever tasted better. I offer Geneb the bucket and he partakes of its contents as well.

The writer in me wonders . . . is the story apocryphal? Did Sisko actually stop at this well, as so many others have since? If he stopped, did he drink? And if he drank, was it with the recklessness that the story suggests, or did he have reason to believe the water was safe?

There's no knowing for certain. But then, that's the way of stories about the Emissary—they have to be taken on faith.

Benjamin Sisko was half a broken man when he came to Deep Space 9 in 2369 to serve as the Federation's presence in Bajoran space.

It was just an assignment to him at the time, something to take his mind off the untimely death of his wife at the hands of the Borg. And at the beginning, he didn't think a great deal of it.

Then Kai Opaka, who was Bajor's spiritual leader at the time, told Sisko that his arrival had a deep religious significance to the Bajorans—though she was unable to explain what she meant. It became a little more clear when she entrusted Sisko with one of Bajor's mystical orbs, which helped him discover the now-famous Bajoran wormhole and the aliens who lived inside it.

Of course, the Bajorans didn't think of it as a wormhole. To them, it was the Celestial Temple described in their holy scriptures, home of the Prophets who gave the orbs to them in ancient times. And by finding the Temple, Sisko had shown himself to be the Emissary of Bajoran prophecy—a messianic figure who would save Bajor and unite it for all time.

As a human, and a practical-minded one at that, Sisko wasn't comfortable with the sacred role that

Drawing water from the well, a Bajoran woman explains, "My grandmother died during the Occupation, without ever knowing the Emissary. I was fortunate enough to know him, and I draw water from the well that quenched his thirst. It is a blessing from the Prophets."

had been thrust on him. However, he tolerated it out of respect for the Kai.

Eventually, a Bajoran poet who had visited the wormhole challenged Sisko's title as Emissary. At first, the human was perfectly willing to recognize the poet's claim, having never really believed he was the Emissary in the first place. But in time, Sisko realized that there was a void in his life—and when the wormhole aliens clearly stated that he was the Emissary after all, he began to embrace the role with new vigor.

Other revelations followed in quick succession—including the fact that Sisko's mother was possessed by one of the wormhole aliens. And when the war with the Dominion was over and Bajor finally emerged from its long series of travails, Benjamin Sisko—the Emissary— received his reward. He was called to the Celestial Temple to walk with the Prophets.

Following the meandering course of the Yolja, Geneb and I see a small city rise in the distance—a cluster of graceful, cream-colored towers and decorative spires built on either side of the river.

"Dinaaj," Geneb tells me.

"Dinaaj," I echo, letting the name roll off my tongue.

It was the Emissary's destination, the place Vedek Oram had in mind when he and Captain Sisko began their trek. I estimate that it'll take us a couple of hours to walk there, but I'm not in any great hurry. I try to picture Sisko and Oram traveling the same overland route, breathing the same mild, sweet air, shading their eyes from the same brassy sunlight.

Before I know it, we've reached the city's outermost precincts. The towers and the domiciles are small here, no more than twenty meters high, but still impressive in terms of the artistry that's gone into them.

As there's no school today in recognition of *Ha'mara*, the holiday that celebrates the coming of the Emissary, children are everywhere in Dinaaj's wide, tree-lined thoroughfares. Their cries of challenge or delight compete with the raucous chatter of tiny, black *kinjun* birds, who flutter from branch to branch with maniacal determination.

"The marketplace is that way," says Geneb, pointing down a narrower street that runs between two stately minarets into the center of town.

We follow it. Before even a minute has gone by, we see a couple of young men carrying woven sacks over their shoulders. From the pungent scent that assails my nostrils, I'd say they're carrying fresh *kurna* fruit.

As we get closer to the market, we catch other strong scents—the creamy fragrance of *ikassa* bark, the sweet bouquet of *y'rtana* roots, the sour quality of *noylib* leaves. Also, we hear sounds—a melange of voices, high-pitched and deep, plaintive and proud, breaking like waves on a distant shore.

The textures of the marketplace.

A moment later, we come around a bend in the street and we see it—a huge, building-bracketed square full of colorful tables, perhaps a hundred of them arranged in a neat and orderly grid. One vendor sells purple fruit and yellow vegetables, another orange and brown festival blankets, still another custom-designed earrings.

One wooden surface groans and bows under the weight of that morning's sea catch, its silver and bronze scales glittering wetly in the sun. Another board bears stacks of blue-black *mekkenda* twists, which, when chewed, control the urge to sneeze in pregnant Bajoran women.

Bajoran culture has flourished for almost half a million years. One of the things the Bajorans have obviously learned in that time is how to haggle. They wrangle over every last lita, even those who look prosperous enough not to have to do so.

"It's good to see the marketplace open for business again," Geneb volunteers.

"Was it closed?" I ask.

"Not officially," he says, frowning. "But during the Cardassian occupation, most of us were forced to leave Bajor. There weren't enough of us left to conduct a proper market."

It occurs to me that Sisko showed up in 2369, just as Bajor's expatriates and their families were returning to their homeworld. Many of them had lived on other planets all their lives, never even having seen Bajor. Could there have been a time in the Bajorans' history when they were in more desperate need of an Emissary?

"So . . . where is it?" I ask Geneb.

He gestures and I follow him through the press of shoppers to the far end of the market square. The place is crowded and the negotiations animated, but no one shows even a hint of pique. Bajorans are nothing if not respectful of one another.

Finally, we reach a shady restaurant with a red cloth awning and three tables set out beneath it—just the way it was described to me. Only one of the tables is occupied by a young couple. Geneb guides me to the one beside it, where some *kinjun* birds are pecking at crumbs.

As we approach, a waiter comes out and good-naturedly flicks a wet rag at the birds, dispersing them. Then he wipes the table, smiles at us and pulls out a chair. "Please," he tells me. "Have a seat."

I take it. Geneb sits down opposite me and orders a cold drink. I order one too, along with a piece of *tuwaly* pie. I've developed an addiction to *tuwaly*, a peppery-tasting fruit, in the short time I've been here.

I look around. "So it happened in this restaurant?" I ask.

"At this very table," my companion tells me.

When Oram and Sisko reached Dinaaj, the captain still didn't know where the vedek was taking him. Hot and road-weary, he allowed Oram to bring him to a restaurant with a red awning in the marketplace.

There was a heavyset man eating *foraiga* at one of the tables there. *Foraiga* was a much-loved delicacy Bajorans couldn't get their hands on during the occupation. Even afterward, few of them could afford it, so the man was obviously a person of means.

Oram knew the heavyset man and vice versa, so they sat down at his table. However, the man, as the story is now told, had turned his back on the Prophets, and he didn't know that Sisko was the Emissary. All he knew

was that the vedek's companion was an off-worlder—a tourist or a visiting scientist or some such thing.

Somewhere along the line, Oram brought up the fact that Sisko had admired a certain valley. It turned out that the man owned land in that valley. It was then that Sisko began to understand why the vedek had brought him to Dinaaj, and to this man in particular. "Would you consider selling that piece of land?" the captain asked, or so the story goes.

"I hadn't given it much thought," the heavyset man replied. "But I suppose I would if the price was right."

"And what price would you think is right?" asked Sisko.

The landowner thought for a moment, then shrugged. "Fifty thousand litas sounds fair."

Sisko laughed heartily. "For fifty thousand litas," he said, "I could buy half of Kendra Province."

The man smiled smugly. "But not the half that holds that valley."

And so it went, the two of them bargaining for the better part of an hour. Finally, they settled on the sum of thirty-five thousand litas. Then a woman in the marketplace cried out and threw herself at Sisko's feet.

"Emissary," she said with tears in her eyes, "how can I thank you for all you've done?"

The captain smiled and helped the woman up. "Don't thank *me*," he told her. "Thank the Prophets."

At that point, the landowner's eyes widened and he got up from his seat as if it were on fire. "Emissary . . . ?" he stammered. Suddenly remembering

a promise he had made during the Occupation, only if the Emissary paid him thousands of litas would he return to the path of the Prophets.

"I may be the Emissary," he said, "but I'm also just a man. Now as I recall, we agreed on a price. All we have to do is sign the papers."

And that, they say, is how the Emissary of the Prophets became a landholder in Kendra Province.

I sit at the table where the Emissary sat, exulting in the shade, and sip my cold drink. Every now and then, I munch on a piece of *tuwaly* pie, which is every bit as good as I hoped.

The young couple finishes their meal and walks away, their hands entwined. A vendor extols the virtues of perfumes with exotic names. Another hawks renewal scrolls for the coming Gratitude Festival.

This is just a restaurant, I tell myself. And Benjamin Sisko was just a Terran who happened to be stationed in the vicinity of Bajor. That's what the cynic in me insists.

But there's another part of me that feels honored to be walking in the footsteps of the Emissary. ●

The arrival of the Emissary so soon after the end of the Occupation was seen as part of the blessing of the Prophets. Consequently everything concerning Captain Sisko's interaction with Bajor has taken on mythic proportions. Representations of the "land purchase" are becoming as common as a prayer *madalla* in many homes.

EXCERPTED FROM THE PERSONAL LOGS OF KATHRYN JANEWAY, CAPTAIN OF THE *U.S.S. VOYAGER*, WHICH HAS BEEN LOST FOR FIVE YEARS IN THE DELTA QUADRANT . . .

I will try to record this as I am experiencing/have experienced it. But for reasons you'll come to understand, that experience is unfolding/has unfolded in ways my mind (still) has trouble interpreting.

Members of the Q Continuum have been known to be paradoxically antagonistic, even petulant, in their behavior, while displaying a control over physical reality that makes them seem near-omnipotent.

I know this: In one moment, I'm standing on the *U.S.S. Voyager* along with Tuvok—my chief security officer—and two members of the immortal and virtually omnipotent Q Continuum. One of the Qs, who I will call Q2, wants to die. The other, who simply calls himself Q, wishes to stop him. Both of them have agreed to let me be their judge in the dispute.

Q2 wants to show me the kind of existence he hopes to escape. So in the next moment, all four of us find ourselves in a desert. My first impression is that it could be in the southwestern part of North America, circa twentieth century.

BEYOND HORIZONS
TINUUM

We're standing beneath a flawless blue sky, on a two-lane ribbon of asphalt that stretches across a sea of green and yellow scrub from one purple-hilled horizon to the other. Baking in the sun, the asphalt has an oily, unpleasant smell to it. On one side of the road, poles, with wires strung between them, rise like doleful guardians at intervals of a hundred paces.

They lead us to a whitewashed, clapboard house with a peaked roof and two neoclassical red gasoline pumps in front of it. The pumps have a layer of dust on them. They don't look as if they've been used in a very long time.

Walking across the house's gravel apron, we see an old hound dog panting in the heat with his tongue hanging out. He looks up at us with the kind of utter disinterest I've never seen in a dog before. Then he lowers his head onto his paws and gazes into the distance again.

There are two people on the house's front porch. One is a dark man with a neatly trimmed mustache, a dark vest, and an open-collared shirt. He's sitting in a wooden chair half in the sun and half in shadow, smoking a corncob pipe and reading a thick, dog-eared tome called *The Old*.

Above the man's head hangs a battered, old black-and-white clock, the hands of which have been torn off and lost. Above that, a worn sign tells us that this place NEVER CLOSES.

Beside the man, a woman, whose bright red hair is done up in a permanent wave, pores through a slender magazine called *The New*. The magazine's cover depicts a couple from Earth's gala Roaring Twenties dancing the night away. As the woman turns a page, she purses her full, red lips and her elegant chiffon gown flutters in the wind.

Like the hound, neither of them takes much notice of us. They just look up for a moment, then go back to their reading material.

Nonetheless, I greet them. I don't get any reaction worth mentioning.

Q2 frowns wistfully. "I apologize for their lack of hospitality," he tells me. "We're not used to visitors here. In fact, you're the only ones who've ever come."

We walk on around the house and spot some other people. One of them is a man in a cream-colored suit playing a pinball game called Galaxy. Two others, a young man and a young woman in polite summer-wear and straw hats, are engaged in a game of croquet on a rectangle of unexpectedly green lawn; the balls resemble class-M planets.

None of these people seem all that intrigued by us either. By then, I don't suppose I'm surprised.

There's no buzz of insects in the air, no flight of birds crossing the sky. Just the smell of paint cooking slowly in the sun.

Once, Q2 tells us, this place was the setting for an exciting and energetic dialogue, a constant exchange of ideas and perspectives. But that isn't the case any longer.

"Because it has all been said," he explains. "Everyone has heard everything, seen everything . . . they haven't had to speak to each other in ten millennia." He shrugs sadly. "There's nothing left to say."

So what do they do? They take turns being the man on the porch, the woman standing beside him, the pinball player, the dog . . . even the scarecrow erected near the patch of green lawn, who wears a cranberry-and-black Starfleet uniform for some reason I can't fathom. An endless round played out against the backdrop of eternity.

True, Q2 is a disenfranchised soul, a dissident whom we had found in a rogue comet. And also true, this is only a distillation of the Q Continuum's extradimensional reality, a sensory format designed for our limited intelligences to handle.

Still, I've never seen such complacency, such sterility, such stagnation. And the worst part of it, the heart-wrenching, insupportable sadness of it, is that these people can do anything their minds imagine.

Yet here they are, doing nothing, imagining nothing, consigning their endless potential to a stifling and unnecessary regimentation. But who am I, a mere mortal, to tell them how wrong it seems?

I know this: The Q standing in the desert alongside Q2 was the one who visited the *U.S.S. Enterprise*-D several times from 2364 on, taunting and tantalizing Captain Jean-Luc Picard for his own amusement. In 2370, he showed up again on the *Enterprise*-D—but not just on another of his whims.

This time he was acting as an official agent of the Continuum. And it wasn't just the lives of Picard and his crew that hung in the cosmic balance—it was the continued existence of the entire species.

Picard, as a representative of the species, was presented with a paradox in which he would be responsible for mankind's destruction by creating an anti-time phenomenon. Q himself added the wrinkle of having Picard shift haphazardly among three time periods, all the while retaining his awareness of what was happening in each.

Was Q helping the captain—or making his problem more difficult? I've always wondered. I don't suppose I'll ever really know. However, Picard solved the paradox, proving to the Continuum that a human, and by logical extension all humanoids, could expand his perceptions and explore the unknown questions of existence.

Ironically, Q himself—and indeed, his entire Continuum—was proving just the opposite was true of *themselves*. After prolonged eons of enlightenment and growth, they were beginning to lose sight of their need to expand, to change. As powerful as they were, they were becoming afraid of the unknown.

When Q2 grew tired of the Continuum's ennui and decided to end it all, he became a marked man— or more accurately, a marked Q. The Continuum recognized the danger he presented to their society. It was then that they imprisoned him in the comet from which *Voyager* eventually rescued him.

I know this: Having seen all Q2 intended us to see, the four of us vanish from the unchanging desert of the Q Continuum. We appear on *Voyager* again, where I begin to mull over what I've learned so I can eventually deliver my verdict.

But at the same time, I don't leave the desert. I remain there in front of the white clapboard house with its collection of lost souls—and so does the Q who bedeviled Jean-Luc Picard.

How is this possible? I'm not certain. But I know from Starfleet files that members of the Continuum can manipulate time and space. I imagine that this is an alternate timeline, then, or perhaps some kind of divergent reality for which I don't even have a name.

Human perceptions are inadequate to embrace the full scope of the Q Continuum. For those rare visitors to their domain, the Q make concessions to these limitations, offering "less evolved" life-forms images their minds can contain, if not completely understand.

"Ah, Kathy," says Q, smiling a conspiratorial smile. "How perceptive you are for a being of such unimpressive pedigree."

"Careful," I reply. "You'll turn my head."

"Come with me," Q tells me, "and I'll show you wonders in heaven and earth undreamt of in your philosophy."

"Shakespeare," I observe. "More or less."

Q grunts, putting on an expression of annoyance. "Was he the one who took credit for it? It figures."

Then he ascends onto the porch, passing the man in the rocking chair and the woman in the chiffon dress, and opens the screen door. A moment later, he disappears inside the house. I follow, knowing neither why I'm going along nor what to expect.

As I leave the heat of the desert behind, a series of smells hits me in the face: strong coffee and sizzling bacon, buttery flapjacks, and fried eggs. I like them. A lot. After all, our replicator privileges are rationed on *Voyager*.

What I see first is a yellow Formica lunch counter that seems to go on forever, but is only a few meters long when I really think about it. There's a swiveling metal fan on top of the counter. It sweeps back and forth, driving dust motes with small, welcome gusts of cool air.

Then I realize they're not dust motes at all. They're tiny starships of a design I've never seen before.

A single waitress stands behind the counter. She wears a lime-green uniform with a stained white apron. Her ample brown hair is tucked into a hair net for the sake of cleanliness.

She has several more arms then a humanoid typically does.

On the wall behind her hangs a pink and blue cardboard sign. It tells customers, DON'T ASK FOR CREDIT.

There are three people sitting at the counter on tin-plated stools with pale blue imitation-leather seats. The first one is a blue-haired old woman in a floral shift with knee-high stockings. She's eaten half of a candy bar. The label says, *Milky Way*.

The second person at the counter is a tow-headed boy of eight or nine, dressed in a white T-shirt and overalls. He's rolling spitballs and blowing them out through a straw. They leave fiery little trails before they fall to the floor. I get the impression that the boy may be related to the old woman, but I don't know that for sure.

The third person is rail-thin and leather-skinned, perhaps of Native American descent like my first officer. His black eyes flick over me in a way I'm not certain I like.

He's got a bowl of thick, green soup in front of him. It bubbles and splashes as if there's something alive in it, something primordial. He takes a dollopful in his spoon and swallows it.

Three booths are situated along the wall, upholstered in the same blue imitation leather. Their tables are yellow like the countertop and striped with light that slants through the venetian blinds—though there's no window behind them to admit light in the first place.

Why did Q lay this particular scene before Captain Janeway? Was Q trying to say that *Homo sapiens* have evolved beyond the belief in gods and monsters, but not food, and therefore are still primitive, needy? Or could it just be as simple as, "There is nothing like a good cup of coffee?"

All three of the booths are occupied. The first one contains an Asian couple. He's wearing a Hawaiian shirt and a white baseball cap; she's wearing blue slacks and a white Western-yoked blouse.

When they see me, they take out a couple of antique plastic pistols and fire them at me. Believing Q won't let any harm come to his guest, I try not to flinch. To my relief, all that comes out of the guns are a couple of flags that say, BIG BANG.

The second booth has only one person in it—a bald man in matching gray pants and shirt whose face has been burned red by the sun. He's removing long, red worms from a hole in his tabletop, but there's no corresponding opening in the bottom of the table.

The third booth is host to a couple of teenage girls decked out in brightly colored dresses and too much makeup. They have stars in their eyes. I mean that literally.

Q turns to me. "You see?"

I shake my head as the fan wafts a breeze at me, moving a stray lock of my hair. "See what?"

He glances at the waitress. "Forgive her. She's usually much more perceptive than this."

"She's forgiven," the waitress answers without even looking at me. She picks up the old woman's cup with one hand and uses another to refill it with coffee. A third hand produces a rag and wipes down her counter.

"What are you trying to show me?" I ask Q.

"What are we trying to show her?" he inquires of the waitress.

The woman looks up and frowns. "Isn't it obvious?"

I scan the place again as the fan makes its rounds, but I don't draw any conclusions. "Not to me," I respond helplessly.

The waitress casts a disparaging glance at Q. "Didn't I tell you not to bring mammals in here?"

Q looks at me. "So you did. But I thought you might make an exception just this once."

The waitress glares at Q. "If she makes a mess, you're the one who's going to clean it up. Not me."

He nods. "Understood."

The woman turns to me again. "Used to be everyone ate in the booths. Now we're getting some counter traffic again."

I study her as the fan favors me with another breeze, sending tiny starships soaring my way. "That's all?"

Her expression turns disparaging again. "Of course not. That was just the beginning. Then came the cuffs."

"The cuffs?" I echo, as lost as ever.

"The cuffs," the waitress iterates.

And then I see it. The boy in the overalls, the rail-thin man with the leathery skin . . . their pants are cuffed. And the people in the booths? Not a cuff in sight.

I turn to Q and shrug. "Cuffs at the counter and no cuffs in the booths. What's it mean?"

Q smiles. "It means things are getting complicated in heaven and earth. Whether that's good or bad depends on your philosophy."

know this: Eventually, Q2 got the death he wanted. But his story didn't end there. Inspired by the force and purity of his conviction, half the Continuum—including Picard's Q—rose up and rebelled against the forces of the status quo. Before anyone realized what was happening, a bloody war was being waged in the fields of the Continuum.

Pulled into it against our will, my crew and I were forced to fight on the side of the freedom-of-thought faction. The war ended when Q mated with a female Q from the other side. Their offspring offered a new hope of peace for the Continuum. Q even appeared on *Voyager* to show off his son, just like any proud new father.

I didn't expect I would ever see Q again. But of course, I was wrong. He came to me again not long after the war's end, inviting me to visit his Continuum one last time.

know this: Q and I are walking along the two-lane highway that stretches from one horizon to the other. All around us, the desert is in lavish bloom, blossoms of every shape and color springing from plants I've never even heard of. The air is fragrant with their perfume. And I don't see even a hint of the white clapboard house anymore, though I'm not sure when we left it.

"Have we been walking long?" I ask Q, a warm breeze caressing my face like my mother's hand.

"That depends on how you look at it," he tells me.

I want something more concrete. "The civil war is over, right? It's in the past. So we left the desert . . . and now we've come back to it?"

"If you say so," he responds, as cryptic as ever. "Though if you look at events with a little more of an open mind, I suppose it's possible we never *did* leave . . . just as it's possible that neither of us was ever here in the first place."

Up ahead, something dark is rippling in the wind at the side of the road. As we get closer, I see that it's the scarecrow. It's still wearing the cranberry-and-black uniform of a Starfleet command officer.

"Why is the scarecrow still here," I ask, "when everything else is gone? What's the significance of that?"

Q makes a grandiose gesture with his hand. "Does everything have to have a particular significance?"

I chuckle dryly. "Here it does. Everything back at that house was a symbol of something. I doubt that the scarecrow was an exception."

"So what does it symbolize?" he asks me.

"I asked you first," I remind him.

"And that might make a difference," Q concedes, "if we were talking about strictly chronological relationships . . . which, as you must have learned by now, are quite irrelevant here in the Continuum."

Undaunted, I take a closer look at the scarecrow. Nothing occurs to me. I touch the soft, sturdy fabric of its uniform. Still nothing.

"Kathy, Kathy, Kathy," Q sighs. "What do scarecrows *do*?"

I answer without thinking. "They scare—" And then, though I can go on, I stop myself and repeat it: "They *scare*."

Q claps for me. The sound echoes across the rainbow glory of the desert flats. "Bravo, Kathy. I

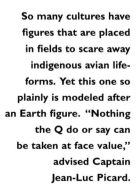

knew there was hope for you."

I hold a hand up for him to be quiet. After all, I need to think. "Who might be scared by a bunch of sticks in a Starfleet uniform?" Who indeed, I muse. And then it hits me like a bolt of summer lightning. "Who else is here to see it . . . but the *Continuum*?"

Q nods, his eyes crinkling at the corners. "So you've discovered our secret, have you?"

I nod, too, finally grasping what he meant me to see. "We scare you. The whole Federation does. And why?" I'm on a roll now. "Because we have potential. Because we can change and grow and expand our minds . . . the way Captain Picard did when you presented him with that anti-time paradox."

"And?" Q says, prodding me.

I glance at the scarecrow again. "And the Continuum wasn't doing that. It wasn't changing or growing. And if it remained that way . . . "

"Yes?" Q demands.

"We might have become a threat. We might, in time—"

"Or out of it," he suggests.

"—become greater than the Continuum," I finish. I consider the implications. "And that scared you . . . some of you, at least. It made you take another look at yourselves and your pure, unchanging culture." Suddenly, I realize what I'm saying. "It brought on your civil war!"

"Really?" Q says mockingly. "You give yourself too much credit, Kathy."

I shake my head, growing more certain by the moment. "No . . . no I don't. We scare the Continuum and that's what saved it. And that," I realize, "is why you tested Captain Picard. To see if he and his kind would be capable of scaring you . . . and thereby saving you."

Q makes a gesture of dismissal. "But the scarecrow was standing here long before I ever met Jean-Luc Picard."

I smile, refusing to take the bait. "Terms like 'before' and 'after' are meaningless here, Q. You said it yourself—we're not dealing with strictly chronological relationships."

Q folds his arms across his chest and considers the desert's undeniable grace. "That's the beauty of this place," he says. "So many possibilities, so many potentials . . . and even a Q can't always be certain which one is going to pan out."

"I thought you could see the future," I tell him.

He glances at me playfully. "If that's so, I can tell you if you will eventually get back to Earth."

"And do we?" I ask.

He doesn't answer me. Not directly, anyway. "It's a long road, Kathy. The sooner you get started, the sooner you'll finish."

Seeing/having seen the wisdom of his statement, I accompany/accompanied Q down the two-lane band of highway, my eyes on the purple hills.

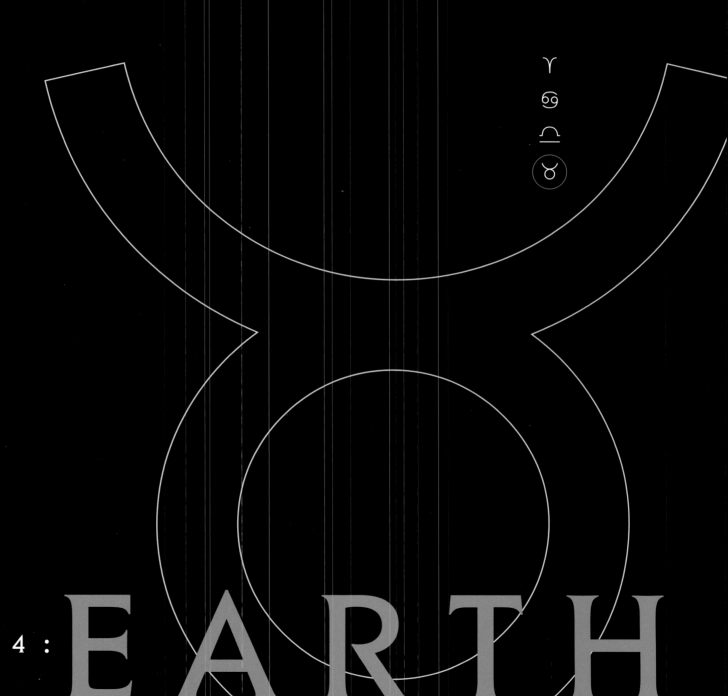

PART 4 : EARTH

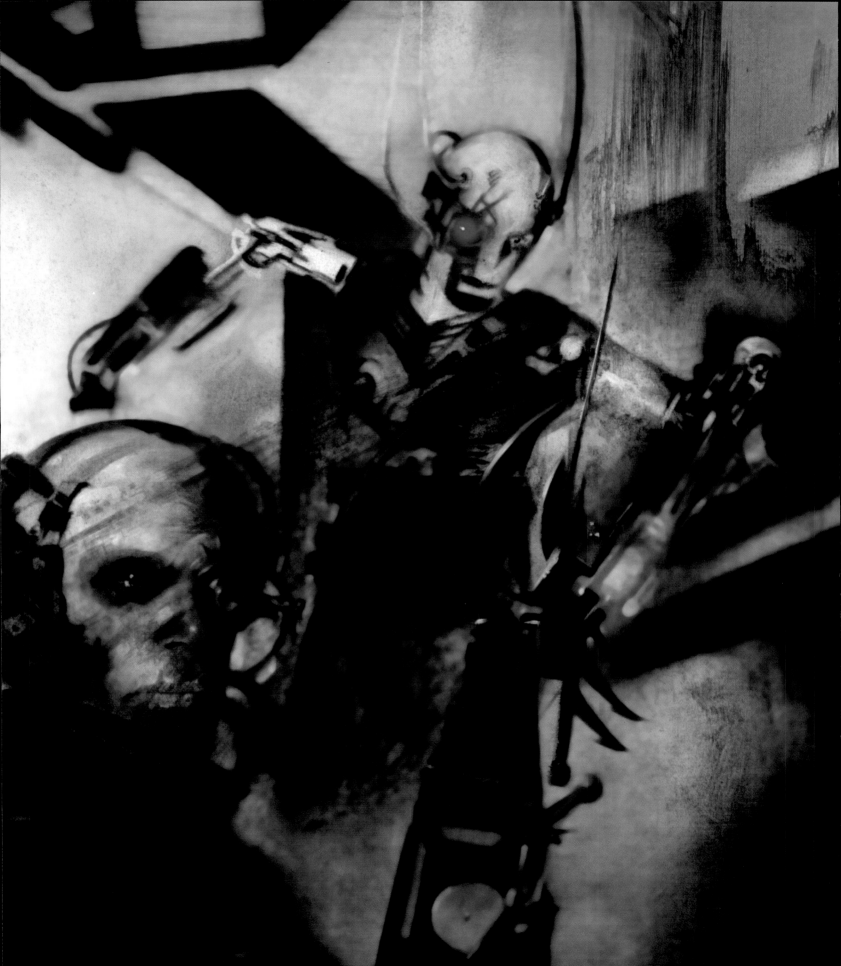

THE BORG
THE HEART OF DARKNESS

Their faces are pale, bloodless, mottled . . . moist in the way a raging fever might make someone moist. They turn their skull-like heads with nightmarish slowness and stare at you from the green glow of their regeneration units, melting your insides with their scrutiny.

You don't belong here, you tell yourself. You're an intruder. Your heart beats faster as their prosthetic projectors carve the shadows around you with a bloodred light. You want desperately to run, to escape before they emerge from their compartments and come after you.

But the dark, armored figures remain where they are. Their black eyes, set deep beneath hairless brows, register your invasive presence but they don't seem to care. It's as if you're beneath their notice.

"They'll ignore us until they consider us a threat," your guide whispers in your ear, her explanation barely audible over the oppressive hum of the vessel's massive warp engines.

You nod to show you've heard. Your throat's become terribly, almost painfully dry. It must be the air, you tell yourself—the stale, pumped-in atmosphere, crushed and compressed by the unimaginable weight of two hundred million metric tons.

Yes, you tell yourself, it's the air that's making your throat dry. Then you glance at the faces of the Borg again and you're not so sure.

A horrifying combination of invasive nanotechnology and surgical alteration, the assimilation process not only integrates a victim's knowledge and experience into the collective, but also subjugates the individual's will and personality. The transformed entity becomes a drone. Extraneous body parts that do not serve the collective are modified or removed.

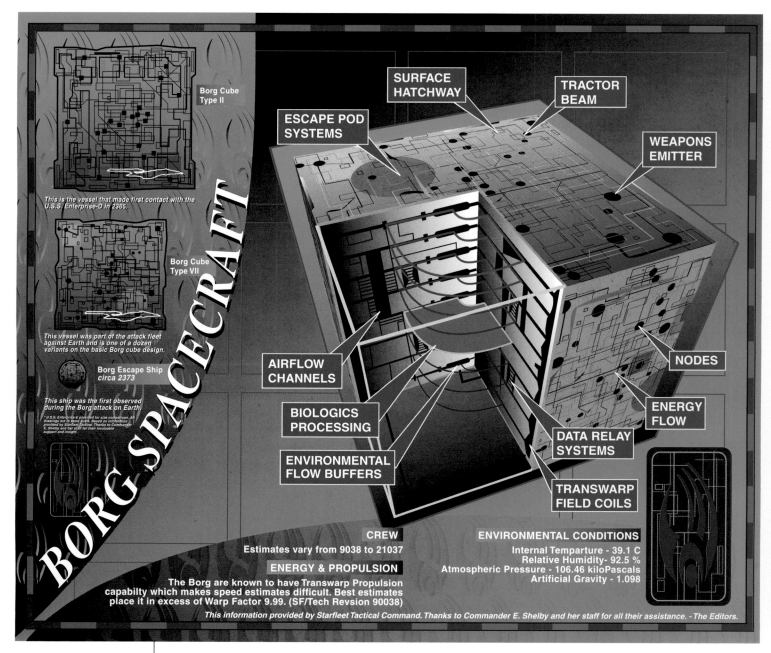

BORG SPACECRAFT

Borg Cube Type II

This is the vessel that made first contact with the U.S.S. Enterprise-D in 2365.

Borg Cube Type VII

This vessel was part of the attack fleet against Earth and is one of a dozen variants on the basic Borg cube design.

Borg Escape Ship circa 2373

This ship was the first observed during the Borg attack on Earth.

* U.S.S. Enterprise-E provided for size comparison. All drawings are to same scale. Based on information provided by Starfleet Tactical. Thanks to Commander E. Shelby and her staff for their invaluable support and insight.

ESCAPE POD SYSTEMS

SURFACE HATCHWAY

TRACTOR BEAM

WEAPONS EMITTER

AIRFLOW CHANNELS

BIOLOGICS PROCESSING

ENVIRONMENTAL FLOW BUFFERS

DATA RELAY SYSTEMS

TRANSWARP FIELD COILS

NODES

ENERGY FLOW

CREW

Estimates vary from 9038 to 21037

ENERGY & PROPULSION

The Borg are known to have Transwarp Propulsion capabilty which makes speed estimates difficult. Best estimates place it in excess of Warp Factor 9.99. (SF/Tech Revsion 90038)

ENVIRONMENTAL CONDITIONS

Internal Temparture - 39.1 C
Relative Humidity- 92.5 %
Atmospheric Pressure - 106.46 kiloPascals
Artificial Gravity - 1.098

This information provided by Starfleet Tactical Command. Thanks to Commander E. Shelby and her staff for all their assistance. - The Editors.

Consistent with the decentralized structure of their society, Borg spacecraft—particularly in their most common form, "Borg cubes"— are both powerful and versatile, and capable of extensive self-repair. No two cubes are alike, and maps like this are for general reference only, since a boarding party could find that a passageway is sealed off moments after they use it.

The first Federation citizens to lay eyes on the Borg were Captain Jean-Luc Picard and the crew of the *U.S.S. Enterprise*-D. Though some of the details of the contact are still sketchy, this much is clear: in 2365, they encountered an immense, cube-shaped juggernaut of a vessel near system J-25.

The vessel was manned by a horde of blank-faced drones, part organic and part machine, each one equipped with an array of vicious-looking cybernetic implants. They were linked in some kind of eerie collective consciousness—not just with the other drones on their ship, but with every representative of their race all across the galaxy.

The vessel had no discernible bridge, no engineering room, no living areas. In fact, its operations were completely decentralized. It boasted a devastating arsenal of energy weapons and was capable of repairing any damage it sustained almost instantly. What's more, its defensive systems were highly adaptable, so no method of attack would work against it a second time.

An El-Aurian serving aboard the *Enterprise* in an unofficial capacity shed light on the phenomenon. They were called the Borg, she said—and their objective was to decimate and absorb other civilizations. They had done this thousands of times on thousands of worlds. In fact, before being incorporated into the collective, every drone had once been an independent member of a unique organic species.

The *Enterprise*-D survived its initial encounter with the Borg—but only after sustaining severe damage and the deaths of eighteen crewmen. Even then, the survivors had to count themselves lucky.

My guide draws me past a work area—evidence, in case I needed it, that a Borg cube is always a work in progress.

Drones are repairing or enhancing a node of a system I can't identify. Serpentine cables are everywhere, like the webs of a colossal spider. Open-ended power conduits spark and crackle, but the only sustained light comes from vertical strips embedded in dark, circuitry-covered bulkheads.

The movements of the Borg are strangely deliberate and unhurried. They're emissaries of the inevitable, apparently content to take their conquest of the galaxy one stiff-legged step at a time.

Though my guide and I pause within a couple of meters of them, they seem oblivious to our presence, intent only on finishing the task at hand. Mechanical appliances whirl and lock into bulkhead interfaces. Components are withdrawn and replaced, metal scraping against metal. The work proceeds inexorably, efficiently, even—dare I say it?—harmoniously.

With the drones' faces turned away from me, it's easier to inspect them. In the eerie half-light, I see the slick, waxen features of a Klingon. A Bolian. A human. A Tellarite.

I wonder who they were—what they did, where they lived, whom they loved. I wonder what kind of lives they led before the collective assimilated them. Were they generous to others . . . noble . . . happy? By their own standards, did they do good or evil?

If they had differences as individuals, they have them no longer. They're all the same now, all Borg . . . all one.

We had known about the Borg for little more than a year when the initial attack came. Since Earth was the seat of the Federation, it wasn't unexpected that she would be the collective's target. What was unexpected was the enemy's timing. Starfleet had developed a proto-type for a warship and taken other measures, but it still wasn't as prepared as it could have been.

Fittingly, the *Starship Enterprise* was the first vessel to engage the invaders, under the command of Captain Picard. On this occasion, Picard was assimilated into the collective, his knowledge of tactics and

The interior of a
Borg cube is almost
uncomfortably warm for
most humanoid species,
and there is an odor,
reminiscent of ancient
hydrocarbon-operated
machines now found only
in museums. At the
same time, there is an
unmistakable biological
scent as well. It could
best be described as
unhealthy, as if the
countless horrors suffered
by the assimilated still
cling to the air.

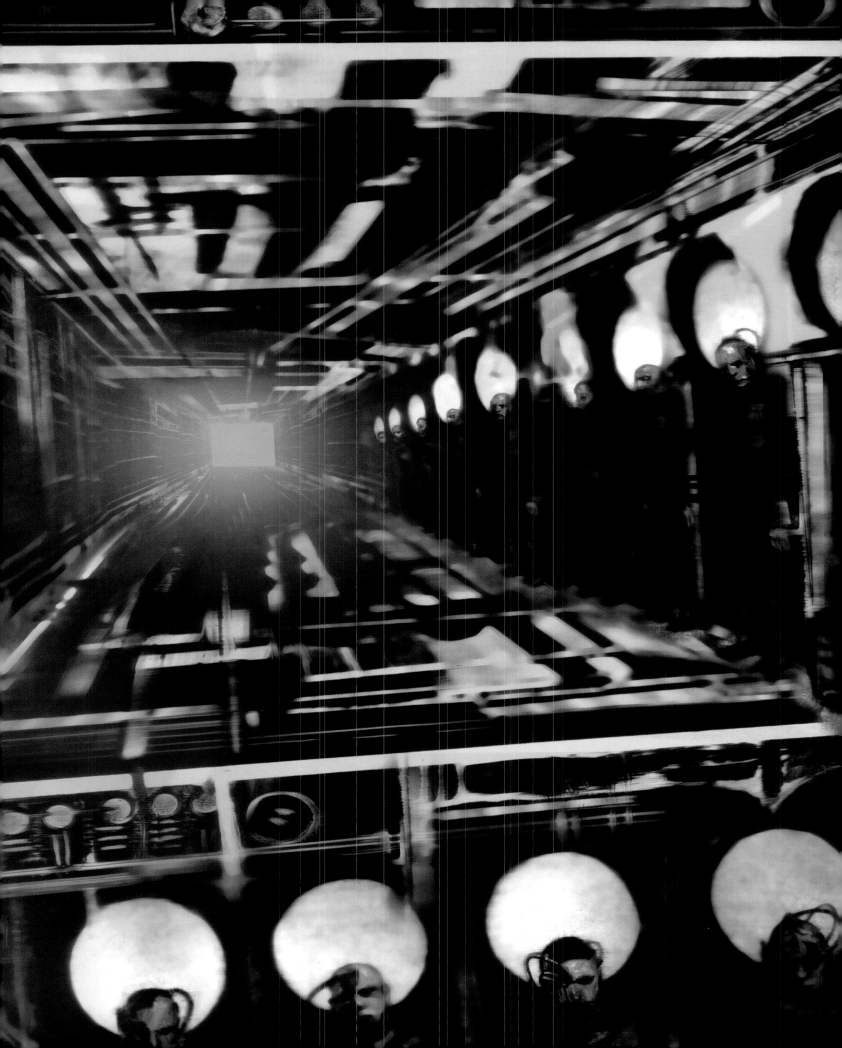

Recent intelligence has added much to our understanding of the "hive mind" of the Borg. We have learned that a so-called "queen" controls drones, that she brings order to the cacophony of information that are the collective processes. Many exo-sociologists have proposed that the disconnection or the extermination of the queen can stop a Borg attack.

technology making the Borg that much more formidable.

The real battle was fought at Wolf 359. Forty ships met the enemy. Thirty-nine of them were lost, along with eleven thousand lives. However, they bought the *Enterprise* the time it needed.

Her first officer, Commander William T. Riker, beamed a team aboard the cube and retrieved Picard. Then, using the captain's subspace link to the collective as a conduit, the *Enterprise* transmitted a computer command which ultimately caused the Borg vessel to destroy itself.

Afterward, Picard reported that the Borg's avowed objective was to improve the quality of life in the galaxy. However, he didn't seem eager to have his life improved by them a second time.

My guide has taken me to the center of the cube—a narrow bridge spanning what looks like a bottomless abyss. There are regeneration units built into the bulkheads all around me, making this chamber look like a dark metal honeycomb, and each unit is occupied by a dormant Borg drone.

The scrape of my boots on the grated surface echoes from one end of the vault to the other. None of the Borg wake. None of them move. I feel like a grave robber making my way through an ancient burial chamber, trying not to wake the dead. I remember all the holonovels that filled my younger days with bone-chilling terror, and once again I relive that awful dark place seared into my DNA.

The corridors we slipped through earlier were bleak and oppressive, the air too densely packed to breathe. But this is infinitely more discouraging. The armies of the Borg are mesmerizing in their perfect symmetry, appalling in their multitude.

The place reeks of ozone. I almost expect to see lightning cut a jagged path from the cube's ceiling to its murky depths.

"Come," my guide says. "We shouldn't linger here." I follow her across the bridge.

Picard and the *Enterprise*-D encountered another Borg ship in 2369 after it attacked a Federation outpost on Ohniaka III. Fortunately, the *Galaxy*-class vessel was able to engineer the cube's destruction by luring it into a solar fusion eruption.

The collective was far from disheartened. Four years later, it dispatched yet another cube to Federation space. It was destroyed by a wiser and better prepared Starfleet armada. However, a Borg sphere survived the battle and crossed time to pursue the collective's mission in Earth's past. This time, it fell to the *Enterprise*-E, a new *Sovereign*-class vessel commanded by Picard, to stop them.

In the process, Picard met the Borg queen—a being who paradoxically embodied elements of individuality while serving as the central node in the group mind. She desired a counterpart who could bridge the gulf between the Borg and humanity . . . and Picard was the one she had chosen.

In fact, though the captain had no memory of it, she had intended for him to fill that role when he was assimilated into the collective years earlier—a plan thwarted only by his shipmates' timely rescue. Defying the queen's will a second time, Picard survived long enough to see her organic components liquefied by a jet of plasma coolant. To the best of our knowledge, she was utterly destroyed.

Suddenly, one of the drones turns and stares at us. "You are not Borg," it declares in a flat, dead voice.

I don't know what we've done to attract its attention. My heart banging against my ribs, I look at my guide. "Come on," she says, beckoning me to follow her as she retreats.

"RESISTANCE IS FUTILE," SAYS A VOICE BEHIND ME. "YOU WILL BE ASSIMILATED."

My guide and I have entered a chamber of horrors, the likes of which would have turned the stomach of the coldest medieval torture master.

Several humanoid specimens, whose species is unfamiliar to me, lie on black metal slabs. Their right hands have all been amputated and Borg attendants are fitting what remains with prosthetic appliances. Each one, I've learned, is designed for a particular task.

Elsewhere in the room, representatives of the same species are being equipped with optical interfaces or having neural transmitters injected into their spines. The subjects stare straight ahead as if they don't feel a thing. And of course, they don't.

That's because their bodies have already been altered at the cellular level by Borg nanoprobes— machines billionths of a meter in diameter that invade an organic life-form and transform it into a drone from the inside out. These nanoprobes are the key to assimilation. Without them, the Borg would be unable to expand their sphere of influence.

But another Borg moves to block her path, its single black eye gleaming in the lurid light. "You will be assimilated," it tells us. "We will add your distinctiveness to our own."

My guide produces a phaser and fires at the drone. The crimson beam slams it in its armored chest and sends it crashing into a bulkhead. Taking advantage of the opening, my guide rushes past it.

My legs like dead weights, I follow.

"Resistance is futile," says a voice behind me.

A moment later, the bulkhead to my right explodes in a flare of directed energy. It spurs me to move faster.

Before I know it, drones are converging on us from everywhere. I realize that it's not just a handful who have finally reacted to our presence.

It's the entire collective.

My guide fires a second time and another drone is sent sprawling. But when she spears a third one with her seething red beam, it seems unaffected. It has adapted, I realize.

I feel something hard and unforgiving clamp

onto my wrist and pull me backward. Stumbling, I find myself looking up into the hollow-eyed visage of what was once a Klingon warrior.

Its bloated, cracked lips are a ghastly shade of blue. "You will be assimilated," it rumbles.

Heaven help me, I believe it.

Then my guide calls out, "End program!"

Abruptly, everything around us vanishes. The Borg are gone. So is their dark hive of a vessel. They've yielded to the stark, black and yellow grid of a starship holodeck.

> . . . PICARD REPORTED THAT THE BORG'S AVOWED OBJECTIVE WAS TO IMPROVE THE QUALITY OF LIFE IN THE GALAXY. HOWEVER, HE DIDN'T SEEM EAGER TO HAVE HIS LIFE IMPROVED BY THEM A SECOND TIME.

Political and territorial conquest are irrelevant concepts to the collective. They evaluate the technological and biological distinctiveness of every species they encounter, and if the Borg determine that they have something to gain, they simply assimilate it.

All along, we knew we were plumbing a recreation—a three-dimensional program created by Starfleet. My guide, whose name is Coburn, has escorted a dozen others before me. Nonetheless, we're both sweaty and bandy-legged from the experience.

"Interesting?" she asks.

"It's a lot more than interesting," I tell her. "It's downright terrifying. So far, we've been able to fend the Borg off. But what are we going to do when they attack us with two ships? Or three?"

"There's reason for optimism," Coburn tells me. "We've received information on a drone who's been able to sever her link with the collective. We believe we can use that information in the event of another invasion."

"Can I have a word with her?" I ask, the journalist in me sensing one heck of a story.

Coburn shakes her head. "She's not available for interviews, I'm afraid. At least, not yet."

I understand. Still, the hope this former drone represents is important to me. Having explored the inside of a Borg cube once, I know I never want to see one again.

JANUS VI

MOTHER'S DAY

Illuminated by my tripod light, the Horta regards me with every millimeter of her rusty brown, silicon-based corpus. My eyes tell me she's just an exotic stalagmite, a strange-looking lump protruding from the cavern floor. But of course, I know better.

I can feel her alien thoughts moving like underground currents just beneath the surface of her consciousness. She knows that I'm a telepath. Apparently, she's met at least one other in her day.

And a long day it's been—fifty thousand years by our reckoning. Unfortunately, it's about to come to an end.

I ask the Horta how she feels about that. After all, it's why I came to this echoing, blue-violet cavern on Janus VI. I want to understand what it's like for someone to be dying after fifty thousand years, so I can pass the knowledge on to my audience on Betazed.

The Horta feels sad. However, it's not because she fears death or wishes to avoid it. In fact, she accepts it with exemplary grace. What she dreads is the prospect of dying before she's discharged her responsibility.

I wonder what that responsibility might be. The Horta tells me to come with her. Time is short, she says. Then, with a scraping sound, she moves—a bizarre process of sliding forward on tiny appendages concealed by her girth—and disappears into a hole in the cavern wall.

We take one of the tunnels "carved" by an infant Horta. While thousands of Horta populate the planet, only the one known as the "mother Horta" has maintained contact with the miners and countless Federation scientists.

I turn to Tony Vanderberg, the stocky, dark-haired colony administrator whose family has lived and worked on Janus VI for more than a century. He's been my escort since my arrival here.

"Where's she going?" I ask, noticing a metallic tang in the air for the first time.

Vanderberg eyes the Horta's departure and smiles in sympathy. "The Vault of Tomorrow," he tells me.

I nod in acknowledgment, having already been briefed on the place. Then I take the Horta up on her invitation. I activate my palm beacon, hunker down, and follow her into a smooth, almost perfectly straight passageway, my heart beating hard with anticipation.

After all, the Vault of Tomorrow is where the Horta keeps her young.

The Federation made first contact with the Horta in 2267, after she killed a handful of pergium miners who had inadvertently broken into the Vault of Tomorrow and destroyed some of her eggs. Thanks to the intervention of the *U.S.S. Enterprise*, the misunderstanding was cleared up and the miners and the Horta were thenceforth able to live in harmony.

That was slightly more than a century ago. A little while after that, the Horta's eggs began to hatch. At first, it was a rare occurrence. Then it became more and more common. By 2300, there were nearly 1,100 new Horta burning tunnels through the rocky bowels of Janus VI, exposing new, rich veins of pergium for their humanoid friends. By 2350, the Horta population exceeded 3,000.

And by 2360, when Tony Vanderberg took over the mining colony's administration from his father, all the eggs in the vast Vault of Tomorrow had done their jobs . . . except one.

The Vault of Tomorrow stretches for fifty meters in every direction, its walls the same blue-violet hue as the cavern I just left. Once, this place was full of iridescent green and red eggs, each one perfectly spherical, each one thirty to thirty-two centimeters in diameter.

Now, it contains the cracked remains of those eggs, the life-forms within them having long since emerged and gone on to become thriving members of the Horta species. As I follow the mother Horta into the cavern, I can't help stepping on some of the egg fragments and cracking them underfoot.

The Horta doesn't mind, she tells me telepathically. Now that her young have been born, she doesn't care about the shells anymore—with one exception. Moving forward again with her strange, rasping shuffle, she leads me to a spot near one of the cavern walls.

Planting a hand on the unexpectedly smooth rock, I shine my palmlight with the other. By its yellow-white glow, I see a single intact shell. It's a bit more scarlet than green, but perfectly spherical.

This is the source of the Horta's terrible sadness— her single unborn baby. Inside the shell, she tells me, the young one lives. However, she doesn't know if the egg will ever hatch, and there's no way for her to expedite the process without killing the life inside it.

Before, the problem bothered her. Now it consumes

her. She's horrified by the idea that she might die without ever seeing her last, tardy charge emerge from its shell.

I ask her how much longer she has. The news isn't good.

live out her last moments in the hope of seeing her young one hatch.

We have a tripod light, sleeping bags, and some provisions. We take turns watching the Horta so the other can rest. Our agreement is that we'll wake each

I REACH INTO HER MIND AND FIND A BOTTOMLESS SORROW THERE, A SORROW I CAN'T EVEN BEGIN TO DESCRIBE.

Vanderberg isn't a telepath, but he knows the Horta as well as anyone. He shows me the spot on her exterior where the *Enterprise*'s chief medical officer repaired a phaser wound with old-fashioned cement.

"He said he was a doctor, not a bricklayer," Vanderberg chuckles wistfully over a cup of hot, black coffee at the miners' subterranean office. "But he did the job. Now the Horta wants to do hers."

"She's overseen the births of thousands," I point out. "Even if this egg doesn't hatch, that's a pretty good record."

"For you and me, maybe," says Vanderberg. "But not for her."

He's right, of course. I'm applying Betazoid standards to a completely different life-form. A rookie mistake, and I'm no rookie.

"We ought to be getting back," I tell Vanderberg. "I want to be there when she passes."

Vanderberg and I begin our vigil in the haunting Vault of Tomorrow, where the Horta has chosen to

other if her end seems near.

Two days into our watch, Vanderberg shakes me awake. "Any moment now," he tells me anxiously.

I sit up and rub my eyes. By the light of our tripod, I can see the Horta. She doesn't look any different to me, but the rock beneath her is hissing and fuming as she involuntarily releases corrosive acid into it.

I reach into her mind and find a bottomless sorrow there, a sorrow I can't even begin to describe. *I have failed*, the Horta says in my mind miserably. *My offspring is unborn.*

I don't attempt to console her. I can tell it won't do any good. So I just sit there, feeling fifty thousand years' worth of Horta memories sift through my mind like many-colored sand.

Then something happens. Out of the corner of my eye, I see a shiver of movement. I hear a cracking sound, then another. And as I trace it to its source, I realize that the last egg is beginning to hatch.

The Horta realizes it, too. She attends the event with all eight of her remaining senses, taking in the birth of her last child with a feeling of wonder and relief.

As I look on, spellbound, the baby cracks away the last of its shell and slides free of the metallic-looking shards, a whole and viable life-form. And in that moment, as the mother Horta sees her last duty discharged, her consciousness fades into silicon oblivion.

For a time, I can't speak. I can't even think. That's how thoroughly I echo with the Horta's last, sweet thoughts. Then, little by little, I regain control of myself.

"Are you all right?" Vanderberg asks me, his eyes red with tears.

I watch the newborn Horta make its way across the cavern. It lingers for a moment by the corpse of the mother Horta. Then it proceeds to the cavern wall, where it corrodes an exit for itself and disappears into it.

"I'm fine," I say, finding my voice. "But . . ."

"But what?" he wonders.

"But did the last egg know to hatch just as the mother Horta was about to die?" I shake my head, rejecting the magnitude of such a coincidence. "There wasn't any link between them, or I would have felt it."

Vanderberg thinks for a moment. "Maybe it was always meant to happen this way . . . and the Horta just didn't know it. Even when you live fifty thousand years, you may not know everything."

"Maybe not," I concede.

And then I wonder if it even matters. The Horta died happy, didn't she? Maybe that's all I should care about.

Vanderberg and I take a last look at the mother Horta, her silicon-based body surrounded by a sea of cracked shells. He claps me on the shoulder. "Come on," he says.

As we pack up our supplies and our sleeping bags, something occurs to me. One of the Horta tunneling its way through Janus VI at that very moment is the next matriarch of her generation.

Unfortunately, I don't know which one. And from what I've learned from plumbing the mother Horta's mind, the future matriarch doesn't know yet either.

Too bad, I think. I could save her some anguish. I could tell her that, no matter how doubtful it may seem at times, she'll survive long enough to see that last egg hatch.

I *could* tell her that. But then, maybe it's the mother Horta's sadness that somehow triggers the hatching, and my assurance could disrupt nature's intended outcome. Who knows?

Not even the Horta. And if it's a mystery to them, an off-worlder like me has no business meddling with it. With that in mind, I retrieve our tripod. Then, along with Vanderberg, I leave the Vault of Tomorrow, newborn shadows dancing in my wake. ⬬

Pergium was once the lifeblood of many planetary power systems. It is still used in many starships. While the Horta digest the rock surrounding it, they have no interest in pergium. According to the Horta, "It taste bad."

STARBASE 11

225 YEARS OF SERVICE

Just in case I have forgotten what Starbase 11 was like, the sleek, black desk in Admiral Carlin's mint green office reminds me. The desk serves as a display for a small but intriguing collection of souvenirs passed from one commanding officer to the next for more than two centuries.

To my right, as I sit down opposite Carlin's empty black chair, I see a silver medallion enameled with a lavender-colored Romulan bird-of-prey. The medallion seems to hang suspended in midair, though it's actually encased in a transparent plastic cube.

Of course, Earth forces never saw their enemy's faces when the two species clashed in what's become known as the Romulan War. However, my human ancestors were able to salvage artifacts like this one from the floating debris of Romulan ships.

To my left, I see a photograph of a half dozen smiling Earth pilots in their black and gold uniforms, fresh from some space victory over the Romulans. The image has an eerie feeling to it; not for the first time, I wonder how many of these brave men and women survived to see the conflict's end in 2160.

The third souvenir sits right in front of me. It's a colorful, irregularly shaped meteor fragment made of iron, nickel, and cobalt. According to legend, the Terrans in charge of building Starbase 11—one of the few Earth facilities to be constructed planetside—were standing around discussing the perfect site for the place when a meteorite fell right at their feet.

Clearly, an apocryphal event. But then, so much about Starbase 11 smacks of myth and folklore, it's difficult to know where the facts end and the fiction begins.

For instance, it's a matter of record that in 2267, this base was the site of Captain James T. Kirk's court-martial for murder. As it turns out, the victim was far from dead and the charges against Kirk were summarily dropped, though the incident lives on as an oddity in the annals of Starfleet.

Somewhat more dubious is the story that Kirk's vessel, the *Enterprise*, returned to the base shortly thereafter and that Spock, her Vulcan first officer, abducted Christopher Pike, his former captain, from the premises. It's possible that there's some bit of truth to the tale, because Starfleet has classified all information pertaining to the incident—but I doubt any of us will ever know for sure.

"Miss me?" asks a warm and familiar voice.

I turn and see Admiral Carlin enter the room. His hair is a little grayer than when I saw him last and he's put on a few pounds, but he's still got an antic smile that smacks of a not so well-behaved child.

I grin back at him. "What do you think, sir?"

"I think it's good to see you," he says.

When I was stationed here as a fresh-faced ensign twenty years ago, the admiral was like a father to me.

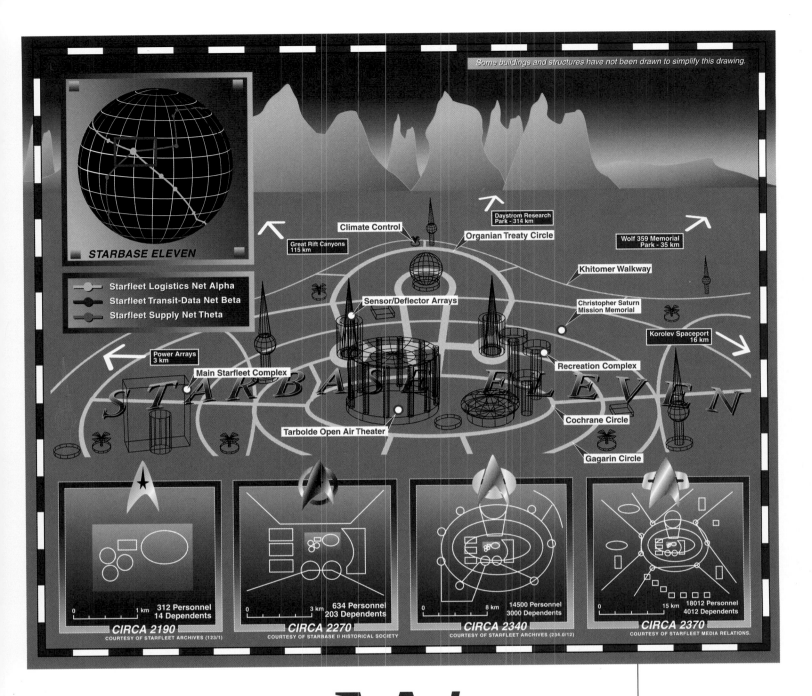

Some buildings and structures have not been drawn to simplify this drawing.

STARBASE ELEVEN

Starfleet Logistics Net Alpha
Starfleet Transit-Data Net Beta
Starfleet Supply Net Theta

Climate Control
Great Rift Canyons 115 km
Daystrom Research Park - 314 km
Organian Treaty Circle
Wolf 359 Memorial Park - 35 km
Khitomer Walkway
Sensor/Deflector Arrays
Christopher Saturn Mission Memorial
Power Arrays 3 km
Korolev Spaceport 16 km
Main Starfleet Complex
Recreation Complex
Cochrane Circle
Tarbolde Open Air Theater
Gagarin Circle

312 Personnel
14 Dependents
CIRCA 2190
COURTESY OF STARFLEET ARCHIVES (123/1)

634 Personnel
203 Dependents
CIRCA 2270
COURTESY OF STARBASE II HISTORICAL SOCIETY

14500 Personnel
3000 Dependents
CIRCA 2340
COURTESY OF STARFLEET ARCHIVES (234.0/12)

18012 Personnel
4012 Dependents
CIRCA 2370
COURTESY OF STARFLEET MEDIA RELATIONS.

Though I'm now a lieutenant commander assigned to the Starfleet office of information, our feelings for each other haven't diminished.

"Walk with me?" he asks.

I nod. "I'd be delighted to, sir."

Michael Carlin came to Starbase 11 right out of the Academy, intending to remain only until a better assignment came along. Six decades later, he's still waiting.

We stroll across the outdoor plaza under a moist and misty twilight. The sky is a shade of lavender I've never seen anywhere else. The smaller of the planet's two moons is caught in the grip of a lively nimbus; in its meager light, the crags that surround us are dark and foreboding.

The air is breathable enough in small doses, but

Few records remain from the era prior to Starfleet's command of the base, but it is believed that the construction completed in 2190 used previously existing foundations. The base has evolved from its original role as a defensive facility into a premier research center.

I can taste the minerals suspended in it. It leaves a bitter, metallic tang in my mouth, just the way it used to.

"Since I became commanding officer twenty-eight years ago," Carlin observes, "we've made it through a Midrossi attack, a temporal anomaly, earthquakes, epidemics, sabotage, and class reunions. And we came this close (he holds his thumb and forefinger a millimeter or so apart) to going head-to-head with the Borg."

The admiral is a survivor. But then, I reflect, so is Starbase 11. It's the only one of Earth's original fourteen interstellar bases that lived to be converted into a Starfleet facility.

generators, which have been gutted and updated at least a dozen times. You can see them in the silvery, four-legged phaser stations, which used to house humble laser emitters, and in the capped-off, vertical barrels of what were once state-of-the-art atomic weapon launchers.

The outpost's ten-story-high administration building overlooks everything, its mostly transparent walls glowing with a golden light. I never thought much of it before, but it looks beautiful to me now. It was a wise man who said that absence makes the heart grow fonder.

> "I LIKE TO THINK IT'S STILL HERE, IN THE FLOORS AND THE BULKHEADS AND THE SENSORS AND THE PHASER BATTERIES—HARVEY HILDEBRANDT'S BLOOD AND THAT OF A HUNDRED MORE LIKE HIM."

That's why I'm back—because in the aftermath of our victory over the Dominion, Starfleet Command wants to mark the place's 225th year in service with a lot of hoopla and backslapping, and someone's got to chronicle it all. Thanks to all the time I put in here, I've become the chronicler of choice.

If you know where to look among the long dusky shadows—and Carlin knows better than anyone—vestiges of the old Earth base remain. You can find them in the archaic black spires of the deflector

As we duck into the mushroom-shaped towers on the far side of the plaza, the admiral shows me one of the improvements that has been made since I left. The sensor console covers an entire curved wall, its multitude of black-and-red screens working like a hive full of robot bees, cramming hundreds of gigabytes of information into bold, clear graphics. Once, the array was lucky to detect an approaching warbird. Now it can discern hostile vessels almost twenty light-years away.

Through the rectangular observation port to one side of the screens, Carlin and I can see the leading edge of the planet's larger moon. Paler and brighter than its sibling, it's beginning to rise from the jagged outline of the eastern mountains. The admiral's eyes reflect its light.

I glance at him. "What should I tell people, sir?"

Carlin knows exactly what I'm asking. For a moment, he thinks about it. Then, as he opens his mouth to speak, someone else says, "Tell them about Harvey Hildebrandt."

We turn and see a wizened old man in a Starfleet admiral's uniform. Carlin smiles. "Commander, I'd like you to meet Admiral McCoy. He's here for the anniversary celebration . . . though he seems to have arrived a little earlier than the other dignitaries."

"Never liked being late," McCoy grumbles.

I've heard of him, of course, though we've never met before. It occurs to me that he's the oldest human being I've ever seen—almost 150 years old, if the stories are true.

"Pleased to meet you," I tell him.

"Same here," McCoy replies, his narrowing eyes accentuating the fine web of wrinkles at their outer corners.

"Harvey Hildebrandt?" I ask.

The admiral nods his head, his white hair looking like spun platinum in the glare of the ceiling lights. "He was a weapons officer. I met him here back in '98 on my way back to Earth." He pauses, remembering. "The base was attacked by Klingon renegades. They busted through our shields and Hildebrandt was wounded. Badly. But he hung on until a starship arrived."

Carlin glances at me. "Admiral McCoy was a fine doctor, but he couldn't save Lieutenant Hildebrandt."

McCoy's eyes grow bright. "The man had given too much of his blood to this place." He turns to gaze out the window for a moment and shrugs. "I like to think it's still here, in the floors and the bulkheads and the sensors and the phaser batteries—Harvey Hildebrandt's blood and that of a hundred more like him. *That's* what I would tell people." ◉

SECOND CHANCES
TRIBBLES

As unlikely as it may look, since the only known sightings of tribbles have been in spaceship environs, the riverbed is the preferred natural habitat of tribbles. After donating tribbles to countless zoological societies, with the exception of those in the Klingon Empire, three worlds were explored for possible resettlement prior to the selection of Epsilon XVII.

Our tribbles look like some exotic variety of lichen as they cluster on the warm, slick surface of a black boulder, their wispy fur quivering in the mint-scented jungle breeze.

My fellow xenobiologists and I feel like quivering a little ourselves. This is, after all, a critical juncture in the life of the tribble species—one which survives now as a mere shadow of a horde that once threatened to choke the galaxy.

Fifty-five of the creatures are gathered on the rock, shaded from the sun by immense leafy plants that average a hundred meters in height. Each tribble is a slightly different color from its neighbors, though the most popular themes are coffee, auburn, and sand. In some of them these hues are mixed and mingled, in others pure and inviolate.

Up on our ship, in special stasis compartments, there are several hundred more of the small, warm-blooded beasts—insurance in case our grand experiment doesn't bear fruit. To mangle an old expression, we don't want to put all our tribbles in one basket.

As thoroughly as we've studied this remarkably fecund M-Class world, selecting it from more than a hundred others in our databanks, we still can't be sure it will provide the right combination of security and peril. By the former, I mean ample and appealing sources of nutrients, adequate shelter from the elements, and a breathable atmosphere. By the latter, I mean at least one local predator with a taste for small, furry mammals.

Of course, that's a drastic oversimplification of the problem. Planetary ecologies are vast and intricate phenomena, delicately and even precariously balanced on the most obscure biological issues.

In selecting a home for the creatures, we had to take into account what they breathe in, what they breathe out, the composition of their solid and liquid waste products, their radiant body temperatures and so forth. We had to determine what dormant diseases and other parasites they carried in their blood. We even had to consider the complex of nutrients their carcasses would generate when they died.

Once we had identified all the relevant criteria, we developed sophisticated computer models to predict the impact of a tribble introduction on native flora and fauna. If the creatures' activities would seriously disrupt another species' migratory patterns or reproductive behavior—which actually seemed likely in some cases—we crossed that species' world off our list. After all, we didn't want to help our tribbles thrive at the expense of some other worthy life-form.

In the end, we settled on planet Epsilon XVII, which seemed perfect except for its uncomfortable proximity to the Romulan Neutral Zone. But for our efforts to bear fruit, we need the cooperation of this world's largest and most fearsome predator.

I take out my tricorder and call up an image of the savage hunter in question. It is lithe, graceful, and slightly more than half a meter high at the shoulder, with a flat head and almond-shaped eyes reminiscent of a Terran feline's. That must be why the Federation survey team that first beamed down to this world dubbed the beast a river lion.

However, with its black, orange, and green pelt and antlerlike cranial protuberances, it's like no lion *I've* ever seen. What's more, I've never met a feline who likes to hunt underwater as much as above it.

My colleagues and I are hoping the river lion can make a small dietary adjustment. You see, since that first Federation survey and probably for millions of years prior, the creature has subsisted largely on something we've come to call a burrow dog.

I punch a couple of inputs on my tricorder and the image of the river lion vanishes, to be replaced by that of a furry, chocolate-and-tan colored rodent: a burrow dog. The sight of one at fifty paces or less is enough to make a river lion salivate. We know—we have records of it.

But there's a problem. The burrow dog population has been declining precipitously, to the point where the species is flirting with extinction. Clearly, that's not good news for the burrow dogs, but it's almost as bad for the river lions who depend on them.

That's where our friends the tribbles come in.

The five of us stand on a slick black rock jutting out over the lush valley where we've abandoned our tribbles.

The jungle below us is warm and wet and riotous with color, breathing what smells like butterscotch and peppermint, cinnamon and hot pepper. Monstrous green and orange plants on either side of a deep-cut river move languorously under the influence of the wind. Tiny, scaly flying creatures that bear no resemblance to birds waft across a blue-green sky, their golden bodies glinting nobly in the sun.

We'll never know for certain what the tribbles' original homeworld looked like, but we've pieced together a picture. Between drinks from our canteens, we repeat the litany we've been reciting for months.

An oxygen-nitrogen atmosphere. A soil rich in igneous precipitates, giving rise to a cornucopeia of dramatic plant forms. Magnificent sunsets leaning toward the red end of the spectrum.

But as I say, we can only speculate. After all, the Federation only encountered the creatures as recently as 2267. In that year, on Deep Space Station K-7, an interstellar trader named Cyrano Jones is said to have presented a tribble to a comm officer on the *U.S.S. Enterprise*.

numerous on Station K-7, somehow finding their way into storage compartments containing a then-valuable grain called quadrotritacale.

Unfortunately for the tribbles, the grain had been poisoned by a Klingon spy—a circumstance that became evident when the majority of the creatures were found dead. The remaining tribbles on K-7 are believed to have been removed by Jones, while the *Enterprise*'s tribbles were unceremoniously beamed over to a Klingon vessel.

It's not clear to us whether Klingons had run into tribbles before this time or whether they, like the Federation, first encountered them on Station K-7. In any case, the warrior race felt what can only be described as a murderous hatred for the little beasts. Calling them an "ecological menace" of unprecedented proportions, the Klingon High Council dispatched hundreds of warriors in the latter part of the twenty-

IT WAS ONLY THE SECOND TIME IN HISTORY THAT A SPECIES' EXTINCTION HAD A CHANCE TO BE REVERSED . . .

Jones called it a pet—one that was capable of reproducing at an amazing rate, though only when there was ample food around. It made sense, of course—why would nature encourage reproduction at a time when the population was short on sustenance?

The trader wasn't kidding about the creatures' rate of reproduction. It multiplied more quickly than anyone could have imagined, until its offspring nearly overran the *Enterprise*. The creatures grew even more

third century to hunt down and destroy every last tribble in creation.

Eventually, they succeeded. By the end of the twenty-third century, an armada had obliterated the tribble homeworld—along with the last remnants of the species. There were no more tribbles—a fact celebrated by several popular Klingon drinking songs. In "Hembec's Sword," the only one still sung today, the singer says he "waded in pools of the tiny demons' blood" and "drank the stench of their burning fur like wine."

The tribbles' story would appear to end there—and indeed it might have, had it not been for a classified temporal mission undertaken by a Starfleet team from the twenty-fourth century. While there aren't any details available (it was classified, as I've noted), the team brought some live tribbles back with them from the past.

No one seemed to know what to do with them. Fortunately for the tribbles, Odo, the chief of security for space station Deep Space 9, took a liking to them and petitioned to have them introduced into a planetary ecology. With the support of his superior, Captain Benjamin Sisko, Odo eventually got his wish.

It was only the second time in history that a species' extinction had a chance to be reversed—the first time being the case of the humpback whales a century earlier.

When we reach the top of the valley, where the sun's heat is even stronger, Varitek takes out her communicator and calls the *Heyerdahl* for a beam out.

We have line-of-sight access to a confinement beam at this angle, so there's no interference from the transporter-hostile minerals in the valley's slopes. Moments later, we find ourselves back on the ship, in the *Heyerdahl's* small but efficient transporter room—grateful to whomever developed climate control technology.

Motter, the gray-haired veteran in our little group, goes back to his quarters to get some shuteye. But the rest of us can't sleep, even if we *have* been going

for nearly twenty hours straight. Zwilling leads the way to the special surveillance station we've set up in the ship's sensor room and we start monitoring the tribbles' progress.

Consulting the green and red graphics on our screens, Caruso says our electromagnetic tags are all functioning—allowing us to tell one specimen from another. Like the tribbles themselves, the tags are self-replicating, so we can keep track of each new generation.

I chuckle, remembering how difficult it was to figure out which end of the creatures to tag. By the fifty-fifth subject, it was only beginning to get a little easier.

Contrary to popular belief, tribbles can be distinguished from one another by more than just size and color. Their shapes vary from round to egg-shaped to elongated and there are considerable differences in the development of their brains and other organs.

On the other hand, they're indistinguishable by sex, since all tribbles possess both male and female reproductive organs. This makes them one of the few truly hermaphroditic species in the known galaxy.

We're still working on divining their societal and family structures, if they even have any. So far, we've seen none of the complex social behaviors displayed by other warm-blooded animals, but it could be that we just haven't figured out what to look for.

Caruso checks the tags' other, somewhat grimmer function—a kill feature. Like much of what goes on in nature, it's cruel but necessary. After all, if the colony's growth isn't checked by a natural predator, it'll upset the ecological balance on this planet and

The burrow dogs' unique society has contributed to their rapid decline. Family groups always travel together, making them easy prey. When trapped by hunters, males will offer themselves as bait. Since they mate for life, if the male does not return, the female will often leave her young to search for her mate. The abandoned pups seldom survive.

sound the death knell for some previously viable species. That would be neither fair nor desirable.

And if the experiment fails here? We keep looking. There's bound to be a place for our tribbles somewhere.

Varitek wakes me in the middle of the night. "Come quickly," she says. "Something's happening."

Pulling my clothes on, I follow her to the sensor room and hunch over the surveillance screens with her. I see what's got her so excited. Our EM tags, visible as red dots on a black field, are clustered differently— the majority of them concentrated in two places.

Varitek turns to me. "Two river lions with big appetites?"

For someone who really hated the idea of destroying our tribble colony, Varitek's awfully happy to see its decimation. But then, so am I.

"We can only hope," I tell her.

Meeting Motter and Caruso in the transporter room, we beam back to the cliffs overlooking the valley. The trek down is a lot easier than the trek up, and not just because gravity's on our side. We're all eager to see if our optimism is justified.

Finally, we reach the black boulder where we left the colony. It still has some survivors on it, but not more than a dozen. On the ground, we find several bloody tufts of fur, though the animals responsible for the damage have slunk off and are nowhere to be seen.

It seems the river lions have risen to the occasion. They've become the population control we hoped they would be. As a result, our tribbles have taken a big step toward becoming part of the ecological balance.

Varitek hugs me. Caruso does a little victory dance. Motter just smiles at us, having seen it all before.

I call up to the *Heyerdahl*, advising the crew of what's happened. "It looks like we've found our friends a home," I tell them, not bothering to conceal the satisfaction in my voice.

Having nearly exhausted their natural prey, the river lions of Epsilon XVII were themselves faced with extinction. It was determined that they were a satisfactory biological match for tribbles, whose proliferation could be kept in check by the river lions without truly threatening the survival of the tribble species.

AT TIMES OF PERIL
EARTH

A tradition of survival, perseverance and overcoming adversity, is at the core of every San Franciscan, including Starfleet

Charlie Katcavage has been operating a coffee cart beside the Starfleet campus for thirty-two years. The lines in his weathered face grow a little deeper as he tells his story.

"It was like any other morning," he says. "Everybody was going about their business. Nobody expected a thing. Then this big, orange beam sliced down through the clouds and skewered the bridge."

The wind off the bay ruffles Charlie's wavy, red hair. "Before I knew it," he goes on, "the middle of the bridge was on fire. Then it slopped into the water and the rest of the bridge half-caved in after it."

Shading my eyes, I gaze in the same direction as Charlie and see what's left of the Golden Gate Bridge. Rooted in the dark blue expanse of the bay, its rust-colored remains look like the well-picked skeleton of some immense, prehistoric beast.

"I had a better view of it than anyone," Charlie says, "considering how close I am to it here." He jerks a thumb at the Starfleet Headquarters building. "I was pouring a raktajino for Admiral Quinn, but I stopped when I saw the beam. And the admiral . . . he disappeared as soon as the bridge began to melt. I guess he had an idea of what was happening."

Charlie frowns and knuckles the inside corner of one bright blue eye. "He was a good guy, Admiral Quinn," he says, emotion thickening his voice. "I miss him a lot."

I glance at the campus and see the blackened ruin of Starfleet's once-proud administration building. Admiral Quinn had gone back inside it, perhaps to make sure his staff got out. But before he could save them, a Breen disruptor beam tore through the building and the ground beneath it.

It took the better part of a day to put out the smoky, black fire. It's said that there were forty-two dead, though no one's sure of that yet. After all, they couldn't recover any of the bodies.

"You know," Charlie sighs, "it was kind of hard to figure out at first. Then I saw all the other beams, walking across the city in big, swaggering strides like they owned the place . . . and it hit me what was going on."

Impossible as it seemed to Charlie and a million other residents, the city of San Francisco was under attack.

Of course, no one knew who it was—no one on the street, anyway. But in the Starfleet Defense building, one of the few left standing, they figured it out in no time. They determined that it was a wing of Breen fighters, put a bunch of starships on the invaders' tails, and blew the coldhearted beggars right out of space.

The whole attack lasted nine, maybe ten minutes—about the time it takes one of Charlie's hot lattes to cool down so you can drink it. Nine or ten minutes, but it created hundreds of casualties, both Starfleet and civilian—flesh-and-blood San Franciscans with families and friends and contributions to make, who never had the slightest idea what was happening to them.

"Commander Illidge," says Charlie. "He died too. And Captain Fong. And a couple of Bolian lieutenants whose names I never learned." He bites his lip. "I wish now that I'd learned them."

I don't know any of the people Charlie's talking about, but I get a lump in my throat anyway. After all, these were Starfleet officers. They braved the dangers of space to push out the boundaries of what we know. They risked their lives to beat back the nightmare of the Borg.

They deserved better.

San Francisco has always been a place where dreams go to live and die.

Until 1769, our famous fog banks kept Spanish ships' captains from noticing the mouth of San Francisco Bay. Then a fellow named Gaspar de Portolá got lost trying to make an overland trip to Monterey and stumbled on what looked like a big inland lake.

De Portolá was excited by the location's potential. Apparently, he wasn't the only one. The Spaniards established a mission church there and built a fort called the Presidio to protect it.

However, San Francisco remained little more than a trading post until 1848, when men discovered gold in the rivers of northern California. Then money-hungry, creek-sifting prospectors showed up in droves, more and more of them all the time. Between 1849 and 1869, the town's population climbed from less than a thousand to a whopping 150,000, prompting the creation of a great transcontinental railroad.

San Francisco had become the gem in the crown of California, a big cosmopolitan city like nothing else west of the Mississippi. Then, as if things were going too well, disaster struck—not once, but twice.

First, there was the cholera epidemic of the 1890s, which claimed the lives of thousands of San Franciscans without regard for age or station. Abetted by crowded and often unsanitary living conditions, it hung over the town like a black cloud until nearly the turn of the century.

But the worst was yet to come. You see, San Francisco was built on a major geological fault line. In 1906, the blocks of bedrock along the line slipped a little and created a devastating earthquake, followed by an even more devastating fire. In those days, of course, there was no such thing as quake-proof construction.

When the fires were finally put out, you could see there wasn't much left of the town. But San Franciscans couldn't stop dreaming. They rebuilt, using new methods and new ideas. And the next time a major quake came along, the damage wasn't anywhere near as bad.

Boothby is the groundskeeper on the Starfleet campus and has been as long as anyone can remember. He has a first name, he concedes, but he says he prefers not to use it.

He and I negotiate a path of cracked and broken macadam between the charred hulk of the administration building and the fluted façade of the Academy, which miraculously went unscathed except for a few burn marks. We skirt the edge of a giant pool that

Once the towers of the Golden Gate have been restored, work will begin on the deck. City officials are committed to using twentieth-century techniques in the reconstruction. In the distance the monument to the fallen of Donatu V is a silent sentinel.